'GLUE challenges us to rethink modern lead[e] for leaders navigating the key post-Cov[i] of the hybrid age: How do we maintain a _ _ "office culture" when the traditional office no longer meets the needs of our teams?'

Inger Ashing, CEO, Save The Children International

'John Dore's fascinating new book scours the modern landscape of work, proposing a new model of managing and leading that better coheres people around a genuine purpose, shared meaning and a freedom to experiment.'

Jeremy Darroch, former Executive Chairman and Group Chief Executive, Sky

'With infectious passion for his areas of expertise, anecdotes in abundance and tools for immediate application, John Dore is the glue on the programmes he directs. Happily for readers, he is as inspirational on the page as he is in the classroom.'

Richard Hytner, Adjunct Professor of Marketing, London Business School; founder, Blue Hat Man

'This is the book we all wish we'd read in February 2020. We needed glue more than ever then, and we certainly need it now. The concept of glue is a brilliant shorthand for bringing together people, purpose and leadership – and making it stick.'

Catherine Faiers, COO Autotrader

'In John Dore's timely new book he lays out a new approach to management where leaders unite employees around bold goals, a shared purpose and a passion for experimentation. GLUE is practical, provocative and essential reading for 21st-century leaders.'

Gary Hamel, one of the world's most influential and iconoclastic business thinkers

'As organisations adapt and reinvent for the Never Normal, the physical and hybrid workplace will continue to rapidly evolve. John Dore's entertaining new book explores the future of work and reimagines the role of the leader.'

Peter Hinssen, Founder of nexxworks, and author of The Day After Tomorrow

'GLUE is a wonderful book that addresses one of the most pressing challenges of our time – how to create and maintain stronger interpersonal bonds among our employees in a world where work is increasingly becoming more remote and hybrid. The book is full of ideas and examples on how to achieve this. It should become essential reading for leaders everywhere.'

Costas Markides, Professor of Strategy and Entrepreneurship, London Business School

'I have known John for many years and I can vouch for his understanding and knowledge of what it takes to bring people together and form expert leadership teams. John is a master of this, a topic which has assumed such importance post-Covid lockdowns and in a more flexible, hybrid working world.'

Chris Allen, CEO, Quintet Private Bank

'Whether the distance that separates your team is geographical, operational or emotional, the required 'hybrid' leadership strategies to re-engage, re-equip and re-inspire your teams can be found in this ground-breaking new book. Put simply, GLUE is a leader's guidebook for the future of work.'

Jim Steele, Performance Coach and author of Unashamedly Superhuman

'We live in challenging times, with record levels of disengagement and employee turnover. In this thought-provoking and inspiring book, John Dore explains the vital role of social capital – glue, in his words – as the hidden ingredient that leaders can nurture to help them create vibrant and purposeful organisations.'

Julian Birkinshaw, Professor and Vice Dean, London Business School

GLUE

The adoption of remote, hybrid and flexible working is the new normal. But like the old normal, no one seems very happy. The solution requires a different type of leadership – one that unites, transforms and elevates performance. Leadership that creates glue.

With employee engagement, productivity and personal ties on the wane, leaders urgently need to refocus on harnessing relationships, making their organisations more humane, and finding new ways to engage and unleash talent. To do that, the single, most impactful thing leaders can do is to create and nurture an intangible, yet essential, factor called glue.

So, this book sets out some ideas about glue: where to look for it, how to use it and, most importantly, how to cultivate glue amongst your most valuable people. It explores the approach of some unusual leaders, and of firms transformed through the 'organisational advantage' of smartly configuring and harnessing talent. Using stories from firms such as Alibaba, Apple, Barclays, Sky, Husqvarna Group, HSBC, Space X, Zopa and Richer Sounds, the book shows how leaders can shape the effectiveness of teams, reimagine the workplace, and reinvigorate their business through the talents, ideas and energy of their firm's best people.

This book is for anyone who has a genuine interest in leading others with impact and wants to better unite, transform and elevate their business. Whatever your role, sector or seniority, this book sets out a distinctive vision for the firm and shows the profound impact you can make through creating and nurturing glue.

John Dore is a Programme Director at London Business School, where he leads the school's flagship executive education programme, the Senior Executive Programme (SEP).

GLUE

Transforming Leadership in a Hybrid World

John Dore

Routledge
Taylor & Francis Group

LONDON AND NEW YORK

Cover design by RARE

First published 2024
by Routledge
4 Park Square, Milton Park, Abingdon, Oxon OX14 4RN

and by Routledge
605 Third Avenue, New York, NY 10158

Routledge is an imprint of the Taylor & Francis Group, an informa business

British Library Cataloguing-in-Publication Data
A catalogue record for this book is available from the British Library

Library of Congress Cataloging-in-Publication Data
Names: Dore, John, author.
Title: Glue : transforming leadership in a hybrid world / John Dore.
Description: Abingdon, Oxon ; New York, NY : Routledge, 2024. | Includes
    bibliographical references and index.
Identifiers: LCCN 2023016206 (print) | LCCN 2023016207 (ebook) |
    ISBN 9781032531670 (hardback) | ISBN 9781032531687 (paperback) |
    ISBN 9781003410690 (ebook)
Subjects: LCSH: Leadership. | Telecommuting.
Classification: LCC HD57.7 D67 2024 (print) | LCC HD57.7 (ebook) |
    DDC 658.4/092—dc23/eng/20230428
LC record available at https://lccn.loc.gov/2023016206
LC ebook record available at https://lccn.loc.gov/2023016207

ISBN: 978-1-032-53167-0 (hbk)
ISBN: 978-1-032-53168-7 (pbk)
ISBN: 978-1-003-41069-0 (ebk)

DOI: 10.4324/9781003410690

Typeset in Joanna
by Apex CoVantage, LLC
Printed and bound by CPI Group (UK) Ltd, Croydon, CR0 4YY

Access the Support Material: www.abookaboutglue.com

ABOUT THE AUTHOR

John Dore works at London Business School, where he leads the school's flagship executive education programme, the Senior Executive Programme (SEP). Born and educated in Yorkshire, John spent much of his early career in the City in senior roles in professional services, then worked internationally in global private banking, marketing, communications and leadership development. He has spent over 20 years facilitating executive teams, designing and producing learning programmes for senior leaders around the world.

He has worked alongside many brilliant educators, inspiring thought-leaders, as well as outstanding performers in business, sports and the arts. He has been privileged to work closely with thousands of leaders from hundreds of very different organisations based in dozens of countries around the world. John regularly writes and presents about the importance of creativity in business and how leaders can better shape the future of work. An optioned screenwriter, he blogs about film, music, culture, the arts and thought leadership. You can find out more at: www.waveyourarms.com

ACKNOWLEDGEMENTS

Many of my colleagues will know of my long-term addiction to glue. Not for sticking, or craft, or sniffing, but as the crucial ingredient you need to cultivate amongst talented people in your organisation. I first started talking about glue some 15 years ago, when I ran the global induction programme for HSBC Private Bank. I went on to create a series of leadership events for high-performing talent groups, next generation clients and family enterprise owners. I am enormously grateful to Chris Meares and Chris Clark, genuine authentic leaders within the HSBC Group, who supported many of my early adventures in facilitation and creating learning experiences for executives and high-value clients. I was brilliantly supported there by Leah Zeto, Andrea Southey and Jennifer Ting in developing new programme ideas, many of which I still wheel out today.

Since 2014, when I founded Wave Your Arms, the exploration of glue has been a regular fixation, finding numerous moments of belief, while working with corporate clients directly and with London Business School. There are too many individual participants to mention, with the recent cohorts of the Senior Executive Programme (SEP), as well as its returning alumni, being a constant source of inspiration and learning. I am also grateful for the faculty and contributors at LBS with whom I have been privileged to work over the past ten years. In particular, those who have taught with me on the SEP including: Costas Markides, Peter Hinssen,

Gary Hamel, Henri Servaes, Randall Petersen, Niro Sivanathan, Herminia Ibarra, Kathleen O'Connor, Andrew Scott, Richard Hytner, Dan Cable, Ioannis Ioannou, Michael Jacobides, Aytekin Ertan and Luisa Alemany. The programme delivery and coaching teams have been exceptional colleagues, with notable dues rather over due to Tom Jenkins, Claire Richards, Michelle Badejo, Jeff Archer and Maryam Bigdeli.

An early draft of GLUE was revitalised by some timely guidance from Julian Birkinshaw, and then encouraged by Kathy Brewis and sharpened by Costas Markides. The central idea of the book – the vital importance leaders should give to nurturing social capital within the firm – was borne out of a class I attended at LBS in 2002 with the late Sumantra Ghoshal. As such, many of the ideas explored here are essentially then a product of Ghoshal's theory in practice – enabling me to benefit from the social and intellectual capital found in collaborative relationships with great bosses, colleagues, friends and mentors, who have all imprinted some personal glue, including: Steve Lee, Barbara Wilson, John Cotton, Stephen Jefford, Chris Meares, Chris Clark, Chris Allen, Charlie Dawson, Richard Hytner, Jules Goddard, Jim Steele, Louise Croft, Linda Irwin and Helen Kerkentzes. Oh, and never forgetting David Laurie and Kieran Breen.

I am grateful to Rebecca Marsh, Publisher at Routledge, for her belief in the value of GLUE, and to Lauren Whelan, Editorial Assistant, as well as Sandra Stafford and Jade Ridgill for their expert support.

Finally, the whole project would never have gone beyond the first page without the amazing support, patience and encouragement of my wife Liz, as well as Sam and Flo. My very own super-glue.

PREFACE

LEADERSHIP IS NOT ABOUT YOU

> The single most impactful thing you can do is to create something called glue.

Browse the business section of a good bookshop and you will find dozens of resources about leadership. There are many great titles, and more published each month, full of smart advice to help you endure the slings and arrows of managing and leading.

Most of these leadership books are about you.

Or rather, some better version of you.

So be prepared because leadership is exhausting.

If, over a number of years, you build your professional credentials, apply the right spit and polish to your authentic self, learn to communicate with radical candour, grow a diverse network, and act out, while leaning in, you might just about survive!

But you still want to move onwards and upwards?

As you progress towards the top team, you will need to become better equipped, using influencing skills, showing yourself to be both resilient and agile, navigating cultural and intergenerational minefields, while remaining entrepreneurial, inclusive, emotionally intelligent and ensuring that psychological safety flourishes in your wake. These behavioural gymnastics seem to become increasingly onerous as you ascend the organisation.

But while the importance of these personal leaps and bounds is often well made, most business books miss the point.

Leadership is not about you.

It is about them. It is about those you lead and manage.

And it is also about those they serve in the business, their colleagues and their customers. They are the real beneficiaries of your leadership efforts, your impact, and your influence.

You know, them.

So, this is a leadership book that is not just about you, it is also about them.

It requires a new mode of leadership for the ways we now work and live our lives. This is not about managing effectively, or making the numbers, or stretching targets, or setting the tone, or providing the vision or deciding the strategy. It is not even about breaking all the rules, atomising habits, starting with why, or moving from good to great.[1]

The single most impactful thing you can do is to cohere others, which means sticking together, bonding and fusing talented people. To do this, you need to create some glue.

Note

1 A reference to some of the biggest selling and most influential books ever published about leadership in a business context. Buckingham, Marcus. (1999) *First, Break All the Rules: What the World's Greatest Managers Do Differently.* Simon & Schuster. | Clear, James. (2018) *Atomic Habits: Tiny Changes, Remarkable Results: An Easy & Proven Way to Build Good Habits & Break Bad Ones.* Avery. | Sinek, Simon. (2011) *Start with Why.* Penguin Books. | Collins, J. (2001) *Good to Great.* Random House.

INTRODUCTION

TRANSFORMING LEADERSHIP

A new mode of leadership is needed for the ways we now work and live our lives.

What is glue?

Glue. Sounds intriguing, but what is it?

In this book glue is defined as: "A powerful dynamic of highly engaged talented people serving one another, the organisation, and their customers, enabling the organisation to grow and thrive."[1] This may appear at first glance familiar, well-trodden territory; another wordy description of an ideal organisational culture that is highly motivated, energising and productive. Who would not want their firm to be described like that? And yet, such a workplace nirvana is extremely hard to find.

One reason for this scarcity is that creating glue requires a markedly different leadership approach. It demands a peculiar combination of behaviours, which are rarely exhibited and different to the typical mode found in many successful, well-regarded firms. This "difference" of approach

DOI: 10.4324/9781003410690-1

is not straightforward, or easily adopted, so much of our time will be spent exploring the nature of this difference and why it matters.

This difference requires leaders in pursuit of glue to act in unusual ways. It is an approach which can feel counter-intuitive: building a sense of belonging through providing greater autonomy; being obsessed with others' effectiveness, not one's own; developing random relationships, not strategic alignment; encouraging failure, not fear; deliberately being unusual, not conforming to fit the corporate norm.

The pursuit of glue asks you to rethink some of the accepted norms of modern leadership. That pursuit is not some random calling though. It is based on a compelling management theory, about the responsibility leaders have to build social capital, thereby creating new intellectual capital, which in turn, creates an "organisational advantage" for the firm.[2] The theory takes some unpacking, so do stay with me and (in Chapter 3) we will examine some of underlying concepts and academic research, focusing on the idea of social capital, not just in a societal context, but within business organisations.

As we will see, a leader's responsibility for nurturing social capital (see Figure 0.1) within firms is a noble endeavour which creates real value and is

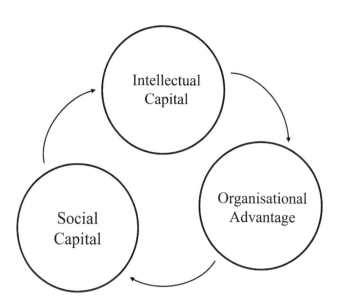

Figure 0.1 Simplified model adapted from Sumantra Ghoshal's "organisational advantage"[3]

one of the best ways of creating organisational glue. But in the new world of hybrid working, creating social capital is now more challenging than ever, and it requires a transformational response.

Transforming leadership in a hybrid world

We now work and live in a hybrid age. As the world of work radically changes, a new approach to organisational leadership is becoming more and more vital. The external pressures are already challenging, but so are the internal complexities of leadership in the hybrid workplace. The nature of organisations and their employees' expectations are continuing to evolve, and in ways that make leading more complicated than ever. This requires us to transform our approach to leadership and prioritise the creation of organisational glue.

Hybrid, as the norm for working life, happened quickly. Initially a gigantic experiment in remote working was compelled by lockdowns, enabled by remote technology tools and connectivity that worked. Then as fears abated and offices reopened, hybrid was facilitated by enlightened flexible-working policies, which were adopted and promoted by large influential tech and professional service firms. Within the space of only a few years there has been a seismic shift from in-person to hybrid working. The debate about the right balance between working from home or office is an ongoing tension, but there is little suggestion that hybrid will end anytime soon. The flexible working genie is not going to be put back in its box and where we have now landed with hybrid seems to be the established normal. It seems the future of work will be hybrid.

The nature of hybrid working threads its way into many aspects of working life, not just virtual or in-person attendance. In the office, work can be both in-person or online, and at home, we can work online with colleagues in their homes, or in the office. Rarely will teams work offline, in-person, in the office all the time. We cry freedom but admit some frustration. Some of us relish the flexibility this affords; others resent the intrusion into their homes and social lives. For some hybrid work is the worst of both worlds; for others an opportunity to feel more productive, safe and in control. While flexibility is attractive for us as individuals, to one another as colleagues, we seem less available or accessible. Our introverted colleagues are less exhausted but the extroverted feel underwhelmed.

Time at work and the place of work have become less distinct. The transition time between home and work that used to be the commute has ameliorated. We can work online while we commute and instantly switch apps to engage with family and friends, who may also be variously connected online at work, or in a social, news or timeline feed. We can enter the solace and sanctuary of our homes and immediately join an out of hour "all hands" on Zoom. Work and life have become blended into a strange concoction. Collaboration platforms like Teams may aid connection and collaboration for work-related projects, but in our irregular physical absence from one another, they have also morphed into a depository of birthday messages, waving emojis and fun-run updates.

Working, or what it means to "work for a firm", has itself become hybrid and blended, with the status of colleagues being variously employed, self-employed, full time, part time, flexitime, zero-hours, interned, in-sourced, out-sourced, contracting or consulting. Whatever their employment status, many have become "quiet quitters", serving time online until time is called on their contribution, or moving elsewhere becomes an option. Others have fully embraced the new freedoms of uber-flexible working policies and now work for the same firm, but from a different continent, with no requirement to ever attend the office again.

Now, imagine being a leader of a hybrid organisation like this? Since you are reading this book, the chances are that you are doing exactly that. Your challenge though is not just to observe and manage, but to lead others through the maze. How do you create and maintain deep engagement with and amongst employees who are often working remotely and apart from one another?

Tackling this challenge may seem a hopeless task before you even begin. For example, in the UK employee engagement remains pitifully low, productivity is flatlining, and retention rates amongst younger and older employees are worsening. Despite investment in well-executed internal "engagement" campaigns, improved workplace flexibility and an employee-benefits arms-race, there is no sign that these engagement, productivity and retention numbers will improve.

A different approach is needed. We need to transform the leadership model for the hybrid age. Not just one that makes us feel less remote from one another, but one that embraces and coheres disparate hearts, minds and souls.

Other books might advocate your own self-improvement as a response, emphasising personal resilience, communication skills, impact and presence, and making some micro-adjustments to old habits and quirks. These are all useful and serve much good, but in a hybrid world, answers emphasising only "self" are responding to the challenge in the wrong way. This book is about re-thinking leadership to be about "them"; those we manage, lead, and develop, and how we can galvanise, energise and better engage them.

To do this is not easy. It requires a radical shift, moving away from a development focus on self-awareness, leadership skills and personal effectiveness, to focusing on how you go about harnessing the capabilities of others; engaging the energies and ambitions of newly formed teams, diverse talent, next generation leaders and those who can best impact the customer experience. The outcomes of this new approach can be profoundly more impactful for the firm and, as an unexpected bonus, can actually be more personally fulfilling for you as a leader. But such a radical shift in approach is neither natural, nor easily modelled. If it were, the exemplars creating glue would not be so few and far between.

So, this book sets out some ideas and observations about glue: where to look for it, how to use it and, most importantly, how to cultivate glue amongst your most valuable people. It also proposes some application ideas for leading, creating, experimenting and deepening the organisational effect of glue. The case for glue is made through the example of some unusual leaders, and of firms transformed through the "organisational advantage" of smartly configuring and harnessing talent. It explains how you can find your organisation's glue, use its power, and encourage others to do the same.

The ideas in this book, and how to apply them, should be relevant to anyone who has a genuine interest in leading others and making an impact. There is no specific management role, hierarchy or seniority assumed in that. You may be on the Executive Management team of your firm. If you are, then you will find some unusual role-model approaches here to emulate and inspire. You may be new to a leadership role. If that is you, then the principles described apply, regardless of your years of experience, or the size of your firm. This book is written for anyone who wants to better harness the skills, energies and ideas of others. Whatever your role, function, sector or position, this book sets out a distinctive vision for the firm and shows the profound impact you can make through creating and nurturing glue.

How the story unfolds

This book about glue is designed to unfold like a story. Before we get into a detailed breakdown of what you need to do to create glue, the backdrop to the whole narrative is the changing landscape of work. We start our journey in the "future of work", which is happening now, amidst a confused new normal of hybrid, remote and flexible working, where the need for glue has never been more palpable or urgent. The prognosis for the modern workplace is not good, with low engagement, poor productivity and close personal ties on the wane. The already tenuous bonds between organisations and employees are becoming increasingly flimsy. If that seems a gloomy place to start, you will quickly find a story about the discovery of glue, and the good news continues with an exploration of how glue can be used to transform your leadership approach and your organisation.

As you explore each of the chapters, please consider the different ways the featured leaders act, behave and respond. In particular, the ways in which they go about galvanising others, nurturing relationships, sponsoring experiments, and creating a deeper sense of belonging. These leaders create much needed organisational glue through this deliberate approach; adopting unusual leadership behaviours and getting the most from talented employees, who enhance their own capabilities through collaboration. To unpack what that entails, the book breaks things down and looks at organisational glue from a number of different perspectives, with a new aspect considered, and some practical ideas for reflection and application summarised at the end of each chapter.

Chapter 1 explores the changing nature of work and why firms increasingly lack a sense of humanity and cohesion. That change requires a transformed approach to leadership. There are some suitably bold claims made about the importance of glue, which are then explored in more detail in the subsequent chapters.

Chapter 2 offers an important back-story, recounting a memorable discovery trip to Hangzhou, China, with a talented cohort of managers from around the world. The visit was foundational for many of those involved, in the insights it provided and the effect it had on the cohort. Crucially, it highlighted the pivotal role of some unusual leaders, their ability to engage deeply and broadly with talent, and the effect that the glue they produced had within the firm.

In Chapter 3, we examine some key concepts and academic research, focusing on the idea of social capital, not just in a societal context, but within organisations, noting the impact of a landmark sociological study by Robert D. Putnam and the work of the late Sumantra Ghoshal, to explain what we mean by glue. Leaders play a crucial role in building social capital, thereby creating new intellectual capital which, in turn, creates "organisational advantage" for the firm.

In Chapter 4, glue is defined simply as "the dynamic of highly engaged talented people, enabling the firm to grow and thrive". It sounds straightforward, but it is indubitably rare. The concept of "glue" may seem vague, but it is based on observations and real-world experience across numerous firms and in the exhibited behaviours of many highly effective leaders. Amidst a myriad of other priorities, the cultivation of glue should be your principal leadership concern, requiring a huge shift in attention, to focus on actively harnessing others, and the identification and engagement of talent.

In Chapter 5, the leader is put under the microscope, examining the key leadership behaviours that are needed to cultivate glue, across the firm. It emphasises listening as your underused "super-power" and explains why your efforts should be directed towards galvanising and engaging others, spending less time "managing upwards", and more time and energy in building relationships across and down through the organisation. The peculiar behaviours needed to do this will often be remarked upon (by others in the firm) as "unusual", but that is more often a good thing, than a negative.

In Chapter 6, glue is observed as more difficult to create and maintain amongst senior executive teams but, where it has been found, the effects have made a huge difference to the firm and its sense of cohesion and purpose. Key moments in the year, like leadership offsites and strategy away days, can be pivotal in setting the collaborative tone for the rest of the business, so the key ingredients for success are set out and explained. Senior leaders should take responsibility for creating glue amongst their own management teams to make the importance of glue visible and felt more broadly. But what works well and what deflates?[4]

In Chapter 7, the focus moves to application; using experimentation to create glue amongst disparate teams, generating innovation, new ideas and ways of working, to better serve customers and improve business outcomes. These experiments serve an organisational purpose, connecting otherwise disparate colleagues. In addition, where the experiment focus is on improving the offer to customers, experiments can create demonstrable value and accelerate the roll-out of new products and services. This is, again, one of the ways in which glue can be deployed for organisational advantage.

There are, of course, many existing and emerging barriers to glue. Remote and hybrid working, individualisation, departmental siloes and worsening employee engagement are becoming the norm, making it harder for you to cultivate glue. So, in Chapter 8, these barriers are examined, and the leader's responsibility for ensuring autonomy, belonging and competence is explained. The role and purpose of the physical office, and what it means for personal and organisational productivity, is becoming an increasingly polarised debate, with different firms and their leaders advocating different visions. For the firm concerned with cultivating glue, articulating a coherent vision for work, collaboration and well-being, this is now a strategic leadership imperative, not a policy call that can be delegated to HR (human resources), or simply a facilities management concern.

In Chapter 9, storytelling is explored[5] as a way to build the case for future investment and sharing the phenomena of glue with others. What is your storytelling glue and what can we learn from master storytellers who engage the hearts and minds of audiences?

In Chapter 10, new enterprise models and modern ambitious firms with radically upgraded employee propositions have emerged, with the pattern of work shaped around the individual. The focus for leaders may need a further profound shift in the future to an even more ambitious goal – from cultivating glue amongst small talented cohorts, to transforming the whole enterprise, imbued with glue. The chapter explores four dimensions of change: leadership style, people development, the employee proposition and the performance focus of the firm.

The story concludes in Chapter 11 with a review of the main points made, some suggestions for application and a proposed way forward for creating personal glue.

A note about you

While this book opened by proposing that leadership is not about you, that does not mean you cannot make a profound personal impact using glue.

Wherever you work, and however large or small your team might be, the most important discovery of all may be that once you have begun to search for glue and wrestled with creating the right environment for it to flourish, you may find that the single most important factor in making it stick is . . . you.

With that intriguing prospect in mind, welcome to this exploration of glue, and a new mode of leadership, which will hopefully engage and inspire.

Notes and references

1 If you need more on this, the "definition" and the elements that shape our experience of glue are explored more fully in Chapter 4 "Defining Glue".

2 The idea of using social capital to create intellectual capital and therefore an "organisational advantage" is explored in Chapter 3. The phrases come from: Ghoshal, Sumantra, and Nahapiet, Janine. "Social Capital, Intellectual Capital, and the Organizational Advantage." April 1998. *The Academy of Management Review*, Vol. 23, No. 2, pp. 242–266.

3 See Ghoshal, Sumantra, and Nahapiet, Janine. "Social Capital, Intellectual Capital, and the Organizational Advantage." April 1998. *The Academy of Management Review*, Vol. 23, No. 2.

4 Chapter 6 incorporates some recommendations about leadership meetings first shared in an article for LBS. Dore, John. 19 June 2017. "The Secret of Brilliant Leadership Workshops." LBS Think online. https://www.london.edu/think/the-secret-of-brilliant-leadership-workshops

5 Chapter 9 incorporates some storytelling exemplars first shared in an article for LBS. Dore, John. 20 November 2019. "Storytelling: Time for a Reboot". LBS Think online. https://www.london.edu/think/storytelling-time-for-a-reboot

1

THE IMPORTANCE OF GLUE

The future of work is hybrid but too often we experience it alone. The most important thing a leader can do is to create and nurture glue.

A senior colleague recently told me about an exciting new role that she had seen advertised by a prestigious university in the United States. She was encouraged by what appeared to be a good match between her experience and the job specification that she had downloaded, so she applied for the job. She heard nothing for a while beyond an automated response to her interest from the portal "chat bot", acknowledging receipt of her CV. We had coffee a few weeks later and I asked her how the application process had gone. She explained that she had been offered an interview but had decided to withdraw her application. I knew how enthused she had seemed initially by the opportunity, but she was now clearly frustrated and disappointed.

She explained that the interview offered was not with an HR manager, nor with a member of staff in the department, but was scheduled as a "one-way interview" with the camera on her computer desktop. Using a platform

DOI: 10.4324/9781003410690-2

called Spark Hire, the interview entailed answering a series of set candidate questions, with her answers video-recorded and assessed separately by the Spark Hire platform, as a pre-screening exercise. She was obliged to pass that stage of the process before she would be allowed to speak to a member of staff from the university.

We briefly discussed how comfortable anyone would feel being pre-screened by some audio-visual bot, assessing (we assumed) one's facial expression, animation, posture, clarity and conviction of speech. When she had queried the ethicacy of the process, the university did make some attempt to describe the pre-screening tool as something that provided greater fairness and equity, allowing a larger pool of candidates to be interviewed, and reducing the risk of human recruiter bias. I listened, astonished at the banal, awful, dehumanising nature of the process. If this is the way the university goes about appointing a new senior hire, what would the experience of being a "valued employee" there be like?

My colleague's recruitment experience was a novel example to me, though part of a broad pattern of changes in the way organisations have evolved and been led that makes them less and less human. One of the most prestigious universities in the world seemed to have no qualms about appearing distant, process obsessed and automated in its approach. In some ways it should have been less of a surprise. We have become used to being automatically filtered and channelled through customer service contact centres, being asked to press #1 to wait, or press #2 to wait even longer, to speak to a human being. In the UK if you want to see a doctor, you need to go through a website questionnaire called "e-consult" and respond to a receptionist's triage questions; then sometimes, with the rare spin of the dice, you may have a chance of seeing someone in person. But our desire remains acutely to do just that – see a real human being.

Working in a virtual reality

This depersonalisation trend is something which is starting to be normalised in the world of work. While in terms of access and convenience, remote meeting platforms like Zoom and Teams, have been a boon for many, cutting the need for in-person attendance and the hassle of commuting, there is growing sense of employees feeling more dislocated and further apart. Rather than improving a sense of connectivity and collaboration, the predominance of remote and hybrid working, making the screen, not the whole person, the primary interface, is creating a deepening sense of disconnection between people. This is not about a resistance to new technology adoption, but moreover, a growing dissociation between employer and employee, and more worryingly, between employee and employee.

During the Covid-19 lockdowns, these remote meetings platforms were found to be invaluable in keeping organisations, their customers and employees in touch with one another. Zoom's share price gained an extraordinary 650% leap in value[1] in 2020 and home-working became the new normal for millions of professionals unable to personally commute, commune or congregate. The sale of headset-microphones, green screens, smart-thinking books for bookcases and stand-up desks soared. Some entrepreneurs saw a unique opportunity and applied great imagination to help fill some of the emotional void. Dot McCarthy, a farmer at Cronkshaw Fold Farm in Rossendale, UK, made her goats available to join Zoom calls. For £5.00, bored managers could invite a real-life goat to join a regular team meeting, online social, or company quiz night. "I feel so lucky that I live on a farm at the moment, and I get to be outside and interact with the animals. I know so many people are missing that."[2] She was inundated by requests from across the globe.

Despite these lighter moments, there were some early clues in 2020 that some employees resented the sudden sense of intrusion of cameras in their homes and the blurring of boundaries between work and life. Meetings were now about demonstrating real-time, on-time, "virtual presence", with colleagues adapting to the artifice of online meetings with fancy virtual background images, blinding key-lights, "touch-up my appearance" buttons and repeated heckles at others for speaking whilst "unmuted". This mode quickly and ubiquitously became the new normal, and while many colleagues loved this new way of working, others were less enamoured.

For those who did not relish the new paradigm of always-on connection, they may have taken some heart from an earlier remote working trailblazer in the US. In 2013, a software developer called "Bob" made global headlines,[3] demonstrating an unusual level of commercial and workplace ingenuity. Bob earned over US$100,000 a year, spending his workdays at Verizon surfing the web, watching videos on YouTube, and browsing Reddit and eBay, while he "outsourced" his day job to someone in Shenyang,

China, to actually do the work for him. His bosses were happy to see his extraordinary productivity and the long hours he committed to his role. Using nothing more sophisticated than a VPN connection and a healthy dose of chutzpah, Bob reportedly paid just one-fifth of his six-figure salary to someone else to write his code and reply to his email. He continued the ruse for several years before an IT audit stumbled upon his "workaround", though his folklore status amongst software developers was firmly secured.

In early 2020, as offices and airports closed, millions hurriedly embraced remote meeting as a smart way of staying connected, but then it began to morph into something quite different. Managers started cluttering schedules with back-to-back video meetings, or "check-ins", then virtual happy hours, speed networking, collaborative yoga, motivational speakers, and quiz nights. Exhausted by having to virtually "show up", a technologist in Nashville called Matt Reid, came up with a brilliant workaround, building a "Zoombot" to double as his doppelgänger on Zoom.[4] Reid recorded himself using Quicktime, looking quizzical, confused, opening his mouth, nodding, and smiling. When these images were cycled through, it looked like Matt had a poor internet connection. He programmed his bot to say as much. His artificial doppelgänger was a little slow to respond, but using an open-source voice response system similar to Siri or Alexa, Matt somehow gave his other self an ability to answer questions, though in a British accent! When Matt then went out for a walk, or took an afternoon nap, he could still be seen to be virtually attending meetings by Zoom, using his virtual bot, rather than an actual live feed coming through the lens. Better still, he made his innovation open source on GitHub, so other software developers around the world could develop and refine his solution.

The future of work is now

Bob and Matt are, of course, examples at the extremes, but their ingenuity hints at a more interesting truth: the underlying trend towards active, or passive, disengagement, with "social loafing" or "quiet quitting" the default mode of engagement for many remote employees.

In a world of remote and hybrid working, the increasingly tenuous bonds between organisations and employees are being further loosened. Amidst a war for scarce talent, post-pandemic disruption, and the phenomenon badged the "great resignation", the world of work seems to be coalescing around the primacy of the individual, who can work from home, work abroad, work flexibly, work anywhere, anytime. But in liberating the individual, it would seem that firms may be simultaneously sleepwalking into a mode of deepening disengagement.

This disengagement began over a decade before the pandemic and the wide adoption of remote and hybrid working. In the UK, and in many major countries, a rush to the "gig economy" precipitated a trend towards zero-hours contracting, the ad hoc engagement of the self-employed, variable-hours temporary work, and much ambiguity about the responsibilities of employers towards a whole spectrum of "non-employees" whom they somehow still engaged for work, but no longer legally employed. New technology and app-based product providers like Uber, Deliveroo, Gorillas and Upwork, were in the vanguard of this new-model gig economy, with some 4.4 million working for gig economy platforms at least once a week in England and Wales[5] by 2021. An employment tribunal in the UK was launched against Uber,[6] testing the legal basis for their deliberate disassociation between the business and its 40,000 London-based "workers". Uber lost the case and eventually their appeal to the Supreme Court in 2021, but gigging remains insecure and unsustainable for many. For whatever category of "worker", there is little evidence of a much-needed first-principles discussion between business and governments about what this really means for the enduring relationship between organisations and their people.

For those fortunate to still be in a formal employment relationship, the contract terms and expectations have liberalised considerably, particularly for traditionally office-based roles. Many employers have afforded more flexibility in work patterns and through the broad adoption and extension of remote and "hybrid" working. For many, this is seen as enormously beneficial and progress that was long-overdue; freeing employees from the tiresome commute, the cliched banality of the office and the work-life balance peril caused by in-person presenteeism. Many professionals and knowledge workers have seized and celebrated their new-found freedoms in recent years, as flexible working has become the norm, while their employing organisations have waved them off, wishing them well in the suburbs. The impact this will have on employee productivity is only just starting to be examined, and in countries like the UK, where productivity has been falling in recent years, the economic and societal stakes are significant.[7]

There is much evidence that the 20th-century relationship between employee and employer is nearing obsolescence. It appears that younger, next generation workers (sometimes called "digital natives") don't want to stick around with the same employer for years, enduring the dull monotony of the career ladder, and they seek regular moves for sometimes no more additional renumeration than the prospect of more "meaningful" work. At the other end of the spectrum, and this is a notable trend in the UK, older workers, who may have early access to pension savings, or have some equity to release, have been exiting the employment market at an alarming rate.[8] In the middle is a cohort of employees and managers with little, or no, certainty of a job for life. This group also has no realistic prospect of the escape route of those who, ahead of them, benefited from generous legacy "final salary" pension schemes (which have now been demised), or from early century investment market returns that are unlikely to be seen again. Those in the middle are often the ones expected to lead others through this dysfunction; required to manage, motivate, supervise, coach, and encourage disengaged colleagues from a broad demographic, who in turn, have a wide spectrum of working preferences and attitudes to work itself.

Many large organisations no longer appear to engender or desire the close long-term employment relationships that "patrician" firms did in the last century. Even lifetime public servants have almost disappeared from local councils, law courts and the emergency services, taking early pension entitlements while they are still available. I recently enjoyed a fascinating conversation with Bruce Parkin, who worked for First Great Western for 52 years and 3 days, becoming the longest serving train driver in the UK.[9] Bruce began working on the railways in 1961, a week after his 15th birthday. He started out "cleaning steam engines", and became an assistant driver three years later and a fully-qualified driver in 1980. He reluctantly retired in 2013 after clocking up an estimated four million miles on Britain's rails between London and the West Country. The average tenure with the same employer (for all ages, male and female, in the UK) is now less than nine years,[10] and Bruce's story of long service is so extraordinarily rare that his last day at work was featured on a BBC TV documentary.

We often talk about business disruption but much closer to home and closer to the bone is the disruption of work itself, and the waves of change are incessant. If staff roles have not already been digitised, they are being automated; if the required skills have not been outsourced or off-shored, they are being moved off-payroll to agencies, contractors and third parties. These modern firms talk about accessing an "eco-system" of skilled workers, from a "universe" of people resources, but those essential human ingredients of the firm do not appear to be embraced, well-loved or protected. These same organisations have become preoccupied with their external stakeholders, investing time and resources in attesting their environmental, social and governance (ESG) credentials, while blithely neglecting the inestimable value of the extraordinary, diverse, creative human beings that have made their firms successful in the first place. Many firms note in their annual report that their employees are "our most important asset", but even in that well-meant phrase, there is the betrayal of a narrow perspective of people seen as a balance sheet "asset", akin to working capital, inventory or equipment, to be noted, measured, divested or depreciated over time.

Amidst these trends of increased digitisation, automation, remote, hybrid and flexible working, and the changing nature and relationship of businesses and their evolving workforces, there is a profound need for organisations to re-establish a sense of cohesion, now more than ever. Ultimately, this will not come through new technology, systems, processes or HR policy (however well-crafted), but through the actions and behaviours of credible and engaging people managers. As such, they are referred to throughout this book as "leaders". These leaders urgently need to refocus, not on themselves, but on harnessing relationships, making their organisations more humane, and finding new ways to engage and unleash talent.

We do not need to become too gloomy about the prospects for the modern workplace. There are many stories, ideas and much evidence that follows to show you how you can tackle this much-needed transformation. But why this insistence that creating glue is the answer?

Some bold claims about glue

Every organisation, whether large or small, has small pockets of glue. It is a crucial factor that enables an organisation to become so much more than the sum of its parts. Once harnessed, glue can create powerful bonds within organisations and can make them distinctive. The evidence for this, found in the stories shared by leaders from many different organisations is compelling. Encouraging glue is much more valuable than time wasted on internal "roadshows", carefully worded mission statements, or repeated presentations of a well-crafted business strategy. It is too easy to get distracted by projects and internal initiatives around Purpose, or Culture, or Vision or Brand. In my experience, senior leaders should concentrate on creating glue, and the clever wordsmiths can attend to the rest.

At its most potent, glue works across functional, international and cultural boundaries creating positive outcomes internally and externally. Customers can sense this, will respond and your organisation's brand (and possibly its growth and market value) will be enhanced. Glue then can be the key factor that differentiates the best performing companies in a sector and is the single most important element that you need to nurture in any business.

A new hope

A few paragraphs of these bold claims and I can already sense your scepticism. Perhaps this all sounds somewhat woolly, amorphous and over-sold?

You may well feel the urge to dismiss this glue idea as hokum, like Han Solo in *Star Wars: A New Hope.*

> Kid, I've flown from one side of the Universe to the other and I've seen a lot of stuff, but I've never seen anything to make me believe there's one all-powerful force connecting everything. There's no mystical energy force that controls my destiny.[11]

And of course, Solo is right.

This is not about mystical energy forces. It is about real, practical, and transformative practices in business organisations that mark them out from the rest.

As a senior manager, consultant and executive learning director, I have had the opportunity to work with the leaders from some of the world's most successful companies. After seeing them up close, I am a realist, not a fantasist. The reality of corporate life is often dull, monotonous and exhausting, and in every organisation where I have gone looking for glue, too often I have come away disappointed.

But where discovered, the glue effect has been extraordinary, and when absent, the difference was stark.

A new mandate

This focus on creating glue is yet another mandate for leaders, but one that I know will have to compete with myriad other priorities for your scarce time and attention. It is, though, an essential mandate that will grow in importance and visibility as organisations and individuals struggle to re-engage in a way that creates belonging or improved productivity.

The context for this new mandate is important. There remains a war for scarce talent. The post-pandemic disruption or the phenomenon badged the "great resignation" (and for some "the great re-evaluation") means employers have to work harder to re-engage. But the world of work is coalescing around the primacy of the individual who can work from home, work abroad, work flexibly, work anywhere, anytime. So, in liberating the individual, these firms may be simultaneously creating a growing risk of disassociation and a diminishing sense of community amongst their employees.[12]

There are at least two dimensions to this: a growing disassociation between employee and employer; and a growing disassociation between employee and employee. The personal dimension is a particular risk, loosening ties between those colleagues, team-mates, sparring partners, confidants, rivals and close friends with whom we might experience some of our greatest and lowest moments in working life. In a world of hybrid working, organisations and their key leaders will increasingly need to find a different way of engendering relationships, making collaboration more humane and actively seeking to make the most of organisational glue.

It is a sense of belonging that makes our work more meaningful, engaging and hopefully, at times, inspiring. Creating glue is not then about a tactical set of hurriedly adopted hybrid working policies, HR procedures, pay tweaks, internal messaging, an in-house gym and improved canteen; it is about investing in leaders who genuinely love what they do, who can take people along with them.

People cohere around people, not around a strategy or products. Who you work with, who you are led by and who you serve is critical to creating the right glue. Ambitious modern firms need to take a long hard look, not just at what they do, or why they do what they do (their purpose), but who they are, and how they make working with others inclusive, involving, collaborative, energising and sticky.

But where do these firms, or you as one of their leaders, go to look for guidance? A famous strategy consultant recently told me that that the number one question he is asked by CEOs about how to respond to disruption and transformation is: "Who else is already doing this well? Where should we look to benchmark ourselves?"

For me, the starting point in understanding the significance of glue was discovered over a decade ago, on a visit to Shanghai and Hangzhou in China.

Applying glue

Each chapter of this book covers a different dimension of glue. After each chapter, take some time to reflect, and then capture some notes in a journal, reflecting on two key questions:

- What did you read that surprised you?
- How might you apply the idea, or concept, to your own leadership approach or your own organisation?

Not every idea, example or suggestion will seem applicable to you or your context. But where it does, please do take time to consider how you might explore it further, or be bold and try it out.

Notes and references

1 Zoom's share price rose from US$73.09 to US$599.00 between January 2020 and October 2020. Source: https://www.statista.com/statistics/1106104/stock-price-zoom/
2 The story about Dot's goats and her quote is from the *Manchester Evening News* (1 May 2020). https://www.manchestereveningnews.co.uk/news/greater-manchester-news/no-kidding-farmer-hiring-out-18183020
3 Bob's story featured in a number of news articles, including BBC News, 16 January 2013. https://www.bbc.co.uk/news/technology-21043693
4 Matt Reid's "zoombot" innovation was described in his own article, April 2020. https://redpepper.land/blog/zoombot/ It was also featured on YouTube: https://www.youtube.com/watch?v=bZ2MOePZuRg

5 Research done by the University of Hertfordshire, retrieved here: https://www.tuc.org.uk/news/gig-economy-workforce-england-and-wales-has-almost-tripled-last-five-years-new-tuc-research

6 As reported in the *Evening Standard*. (19 February 2021) "Uber loses Supreme Court appeal as court rules drivers are workers with rights to minimum wage." https://www.standard.co.uk/news/uk/uber-workers-rights-supreme-court-ruling-b920444.html. A copy of the judgement of The Supreme Court, with its definition of "worker" is available at: https://www.supremecourt.uk/press-summary/uksc-2019-0029.html

7 Source: https://www.ons.gov.uk/ In 2019, the UK's output per hour worked was lower than the US and France and compared to the largest G7 countries' average (excluding the UK), output per worker was 13% above the UK in 2019.

8 Source: https://www.ons.gov.uk/ In 2019, 13.8% of people aged 50 years were economically inactive and at age 64 years over half (51.9%) were economically inactive. Source: https://www.ons.gov.uk/

9 Bruce Parkin's story was featured in a BBC documentary about First Great Western trains, first broadcast in 2013. Retrieved from: https://www.dailymail.co.uk/news/article-2385224/Britains-longest-serving-train-driver-retires-52-years-5-mins-late-final-stop.html

10 In 2017, the average tenure for someone in a job in the UK was just under nine years, a figure unchanged since 1997, according to the OECD. The average job tenure of under-25s had fallen slightly, from 1.8 years to 1.7 years. Source: https://www.cipd.co.uk/Images/7904-megatrends-insecurity-report-final_tcm18-61556.pdf

11 The feature film *Star Wars, A New Hope* was written and directed by George Lucas and released in cinemas in 1977. According to the lore created by Lucas, The Force was an energy field created by all life that connected everything in the universe and was known by a variety of names throughout galactic history. It has though, absolutely nothing to do with glue.

12 Porath, Christine and Piñeyro Sublett, Carla. (26 August 2022) "Rekindling a Sense of Community at Work." *Harvard Business Review*. Abstract: During the 2020/21 pandemic, many of us became more isolated than before. Community, which the authors define as a group of individuals who share a mutual concern for one another's welfare, has proven challenging to cultivate, especially for those working virtually. Available at: https://hbr.org/2022/08/rekindling-a-sense-of-community-at-work

2

DISCOVERING GLUE

Discovering the profound impact created by leaders who understood and harnessed glue.

Shanghai, China, October 2010

There was something that felt a little odd that morning in Shanghai. We took a bus from the hotel, crossing the old town without many hold-ups. All the traffic lights seemed to turn red to green. We took photos from The Bund riverside walkway, staring across to the Pudong district to see the mile-high skyscrapers and everything was eerily calm. A city with over 20 million citizens was somehow way too quiet? It took a while for the penny to drop, before one of our local hosts told us the story. During the Shanghai World Expo,[1] the local mayor had instructed that there would be no major building or traffic disruption. This great international city, an economic gateway to China, would appear to all visitors as if "finished",

DOI: 10.4324/9781003410690-3

and not as a work in progress. So, there were no cranes in sight. No building works. No dug-up roads. The skyscrapers that were unfinished were covered in acres of plastic sheeting, with enormous realistic facades.

It would be impossible for this city-wide discipline to be adhered to in any major European or North American City. The emphatic motto for Shanghai was: "Better City, Better Life" and here, the mayor's rules ruled. China was the fastest growing economy in the world, and Shanghai was at the heart of a new burgeoning unfettered capitalism, but things were done in a certain Party-determined way, and when a government official said hit the pause button, the city simply went on hold. It was unnerving in a way to see the imposition of such sudden order, at such scale and, at the same time, as I looked across the river and the gigantic barges passed below without sounding their horns, somehow it all seemed rather surreal.

Maybe it was this early "aha moment" that was the trigger? I needed to better make sense of things in plain sight: to be more alert on this trip, to spot patterns, to think smarter, and to make better sense of what we were observing and hearing. Appropriately, the theme of the programme in China was "dongcha" – a Chinese word meaning insight – and from that morning onwards, the moments of dongcha came thick and fast.

As we crossed the park of the Shanghai World Expo, the shiny zero-emission e-bus had broken down on a slope outside the enormous China Pavilion. I was sat at the front of an elongated driverless cart with 50 mid-career managers from various parts of the world. Some 50 million visitors attended the Shanghai World Expo in just over four months during 2010 and although the day we visited was described by our hosts as a "quiet day" some 300,000 guests still passed through the park. Like us, they endured the lengthy queues and cloying humidity to file through the security gates and explore the vast global showcase. Some local visitors stopped and stared at us with much amusement, taking photographs of our multinational cohort, as we sat stuck on the bus, somewhat pathetically, on an incline, waiting for an engineer to get us re-started. As one of the organisers of the visit, the group teased and heckled me gently, as we finally disembarked, heading on foot in different directions to explore the park.

Each participant on that visit to Shanghai had been personally and carefully chosen by Chris Meares, the CEO of HSBC's private banking business, from amongst the most talented people in the organisation. Meares was the sponsor of an immersive learning programme and a week of lectures, workshops, tours and client visits in China. The cohort were known within the business as members of the High-Performance Development Programme, or HPDP, and securing an invitation to participate in that cohort from amongst an organisation of over 5,000 employees was a significant career accomplishment in itself.

Bannister needed some glue

The HPDP programme was not a product of the HR department, who had little involvement, but was the brainchild of Meares' predecessor, the global CEO for the business, Clive Bannister. Bannister was the son of Roger Bannister, a middle-distance runner, who became world-famous as the first man to run a mile in under four minutes. Clive was a tall bespectacled figure, and an impressive public-speaker, whose imprint on the business was significant. HSBC's private banking business was an amalgam of various banking and trust companies, bought by the behemoth group during the previous decade, including Republic National Bank, Samuel Montagu, Trinkaus & Burkhardt, Guyerzeller, the Bank of Bermuda and Credit Commercial de France. In the early 2000s, this collection of acquired entities and trust companies was brought under a new unified HSBC brand, though much more was needed to bind them together than a shared logo. The various entities were profitable, with significant client assets under management, and a strong base in key wealth hubs like Switzerland and Asia, but the potential was there for the business to be worth much more than a sum of its parts.

For Bannister, creating value through providing a joined-up offer to global private clients and family business owners was a major challenge. He was looking for ways other than corporate governance and his management team's efforts to encourage client referrals and collaboration across the various entities. He saw that one of the smart ways of doing that was by taking personal ownership of talent development and co-ordinating that globally. He initiated a programme of new hire induction where, on a quarterly basis (coinciding with the scheduled Board meetings), all new senior hires attended a four-day global workshop, which was led and facilitated by members of his executive team. He would attend the last morning of the workshop and put the new hires to work on some thorny business problem, sourcing fresh ideas and debating the proposals with them. From the off, he wanted new talent to know that, regardless of where they started with the organisation, they were part of a joined-up globally led organisation and that he, personally, valued their view.

A few years later, the HPDP group brought together in China were beneficiaries of Bannister's early decision to better harness talent. The China cohort was made up of major fee earners, working for high-net worth clients and their families. Others were gifted functional staff, managing credit, risk, operations, technology and compliance. All were committed to making the business a great organisation for their clients. Competition for a place on a trip like this was fierce, and participants were selected from every continent, bringing together a diverse group from different backgrounds, cultures, workstyles and disciplines. The HPDP participant group was refreshed every couple of years, with talent coming in and others (who may have made less of the opportunity) leaving the cohort.

The China cohort

The previous two years had been a difficult time for global financial services, but Chris Meares (who had succeeded Bannister in 2006) was committed to continuing to invest in developing talent and, despite turbulent markets and cost pressures, he was also determined to bring the whole HPDP group together, at least once a year. We had worked together on a plan for some time to run a programme in China. Our objective was to connect the participants with their colleagues in Shanghai, visit the Expo and also spend some time with corporate customers, clients, and senior executives from global businesses in the region. China was a major market for HSBC, the fastest growing economy in the world, and the HPDP cohort (many of whom had probably only ever visited Hong Kong in the region) needed to understand the China growth story better. Meares wanted them to be more articulate about the market opportunity for their clients and investment management colleagues.

One of the best ways to do this was to get the cohort to meet and talk with business leaders running firms in the region. I had contacted a number of organisations ahead of the trip, including taking a rather ballsy punt and emailing Steve Jobs at Apple to ask if he could connect us with his team leading their operations in China. His quick response, sent from his iPad, was suitably blunt:

"No interest. Thanks for thinking of us." Steve

Jobs' email remains framed on my office wall. But our other outreach was more successful, including securing a visit and private tour of the hard to access Alibaba headquarters, in the evocative lakeside setting in Hangzhou.

Before heading to Hangzhou, we met Helen Wong, the head of HSBC's business in China. She ran a significant commercial and personal banking network, with over 120 HSBC branches in the major cities, though she offered a reality-check in case we were impressed, as her Chinese competitor banks had around 100,000 branches in the country. Even an organisation as globally significant as HSBC is a relative minnow in mainland China. We met a number of Shanghai-based companies and, at face value, much seemed familiar, but Helen helped us notice that much was also very different. She told us that acclimatising to business in China was about realising that similarities are deliberate, not accidental and, where found, are well chosen. Practices, approaches and ways of working were often cherry picked from western firms, but much that was different was that way for a distinctly Chinese reason. It was a helpful insight as we continued our tour.

A couple of days later we took an unglamorous three-hour bus journey from Shanghai across country to Hangzhou. Today you can take the bullet train in about 45 minutes. We had arranged to meet the team at Alibaba Group, visit the Campus and to hear the first-hand experience of former Alibaba President, Savio Kwan. We were given a vivid sense of the importance of company culture and how, when that culture was embodied by the CEO and cultivated deeply into the organisation, extraordinary things could happen in the business. In other words, in Hangzhou we discovered a story about creating glue.

Alibaba

Hangzhou is an extraordinary place, more like Zurich, or Lausanne than Beijing, or Shenzhen. A picturesque university city bordered by the Yangtze River and surrounded by green hills, it seems timeless, ancient and curiously modern. Its elegant houses look out over lakeside parks and smart cafes, while e-scooters fly along tree-lined boulevards. Behind the enormous, restored Lei Feng Pagoda, the hazy light glints off the frontage of the Bugatti, Ferrari and Porsche garages. As we arrived, the bold reality of "Communist" China in 2010 was brought into dramatic focus.

Turning off the main road, we headed through a forested park and into the entrance of the Alibaba Campus. The company headquarters is designed like a university campus, a 2-million square foot head-office building, but with an enormous Starbucks, library, bookstore and organic grocery store. Alibaba was then only just a decade old but had already acquired over 350 million customers through its massively popular online brands Alibaba and Taobao. We each took in the scope and scale of the place – not just admiring the smart offices, but also meeting some of the 13,000 young men and women working long hours for what they called humbly an "internet business". The employees had lunch together, within the vast aircraft hanger of a canteen, which serves thousands of covers a day, across different shifts.

We sat in the tiered lecture-theatre "briefing room" and watched the floor-to-ceiling video wall, flashing with real-time data feeds. Our hosts shared how Alibaba could supply pretty much any item bought through Alibaba in just a matter of hours to pretty much any address, anywhere in China. Their ambition was to further invest in a vast network of local fulfilment centres and by using predictive purchase algorithms and smart inventory models, be able to complete order-to-delivery times in minutes, not hours. In 2010, as we fiddled taking notes on a Blackberry, this sounded like science fiction. The campus and the business model were impressive, but it was the culture and feel of the place that was most memorable.

Savio Kwan talks about Jack

Our keynote speaker was Savio Kwan, who was then a non-executive director of Alibaba. He was a passionate advocate for the enduring culture and future potential of (what was then) the fastest growing enterprise in the world. Savio had been hired by Alibaba CEO Jack Ma from GE – an organisation Ma admired greatly, particularly for the leadership of his namesake CEO Jack Walsh. Rather than dwell on the scale and scope of the vast contemporary operation, Savio spent much time on the importance of the background story of Alibaba and its formative days. The business was deliberately set up like a Silicon Valley style start-up venture. Whilst Hewlett Packard, Microsoft and Apple were famously founded by entrepreneurs in suburban US garages, Alibaba was born in Jack Ma's flat, though it was the same culture of innovation from Silicon Valley that Ma was keen to import and build.

Savio retold the Alibaba story, not as some romanticised business myth, but as a somewhat chaotic, youthful adventure. It was February 1999 when Ma asked a group of friends to gather in his second-floor apartment at the Lakeside Gardens building in Hangzhou. At the beginning of that year, China only had two million internet users and computers were very expensive, but Ma was undeterred. He was enormously ambitious, and described how they would launch Alibaba, build the business from scratch and float within three years, making him and his close-knit founder group extraordinarily rich in the process. The original founders huddled together with Jack were his wife Cathy, plus 16 others; six women and ten men – a small group of collaborators ready to make their own dent in the universe.

Ma stood up and addressed the founder group in his flat:

> Our competitors are not Chinese websites, but overseas websites. They are not in China, but in America's Silicon Valley. So first, we should position Alibaba as a global website, not just a domestic website. We need to learn the hard-working spirit of Silicon Valley. This is the reason we dare to compete with the Americans. If we are a good team and know what we want to do, one of us can defeat ten of them. We can beat big famous companies because of our innovative spirit. So don't worry. The dream of the internet won't burst. We will have to pay a painful price in the next three to five years. It is the only way we can succeed and so, Alibaba will IPO in 2002.[2]

From the off, Ma sought to galvanise a core group of talented people around an ambitious goal. To his enduring credit, he made every one of the team a shareholder from day one. He got them excited about the future, telling them that the rewards would be great, but also warning them they should leave immediately if they expected a "9 to 5" commitment. A visiting executive from the global investment bank Goldman Sachs saw the early days set-up in the flat: a crowded mess of people, working night and day, eating, working, and sleeping on the floor. Within a few months Goldman became an early investor.

Ma was not just a workaholic; he was also quirky and unconventional in the ways he sought to bind together the team. Savio showed photos of the founders doing headstands against the wall of the apartment – encouraged while upside-down "to see the world from a different point of view". Ma's management style was a strange fusion of adopted US business practices and ancient Chinese wisdom. He was CEO but also known as "the teacher". His love of martial arts helped to create a tradition where employees used aliases inspired by kung fu novels. His own nickname was Feng Qing Yang, which means "Refreshing Wind" – the name of a reclusive swordsman in a kung fu novel.[3]

Savio shared something of his own part of the Alibaba story – where tough decisions needed to be made – as the venture went through growing pains, and he talked about the strength of the founder values, as well as some jaw-dropping tales about the wealth generated amongst that original founder group. The consistent thread through the whole tale was the unusual leadership style and impact of Ma: straightforward, but enigmatic, playful, but deeply serious about hard work, and unequivocal on business ethics. Duncan Clark, author of *Alibaba: The House That Jack Ma Built*, describes Ma as a having:

> a unique Chinese combination of blarney and chutzpah. Like another charismatic tech founder Steve Jobs, he is able to create his own "reality disruption field" and his communication style is so effective because his message is so easy to agree with, remember and digest.[4]

As we were guided through the offices on the Alibaba campus, the original values on which the business was founded by Ma were visible everywhere. Values were fundamental to the firm from the outset, with focus on the customer the priority, ahead of shareholders and employees. Many of us work for organisations where the importance of "values" is banded around by the HR manager or posted on the CEO's intranet site. Throughout the Alibaba HQ, values are posted on every workstation, along corridors, on the walls, on printed literature, on screensavers, in the bathroom, on the ceiling, and on the floors. We also saw those values imprinted more deeply, with the whole place and the people you meet imbued with them. The campus exudes a distinctive corporate culture: irreverent, playful, and cheeky, with the use of adopted nicknames still maintained, with top performing employees called "bing wang" meaning Soldier Kings.[5]

The combination of core values, a visible culture of hard work (which is unashamedly one that will mean long hours) and an unconventional leadership style was a heady brew. My notes at the time were a simple summation: "Strong values, crazy hours, unusual leadership."

Today, Alibaba dominates the eBay-style self-trading market across China and, while today, in very different political circumstances, Jack Ma is a lower-profile figure in China and abroad, his 25-year legacy is a US$125 billion revenue enterprise. His own personal wealth, born out of those early days doing headstands in his flat, is estimated at US$35 billion and the founder group each became enormously wealthy when the company's shares were offered on the New York Stock Exchange and the subsequent explosion of digital commerce in China.

The Hangzhou effect

Back in Shanghai, Meares led a conversation with the group about what they had seen and heard during their week in China. The participants had enjoyed a rare experience, full of insights, interesting customer conversations, inspiring talks, workshops and an exploration of Chinese trends and themes. There was much to ponder on what the market meant and could mean for business in the future. There were many highlights, but the conversation often returned to the Alibaba visit. Before departing they spent some time to work through and capture the learning, mapping ideas, outcomes and new opportunities.

Meares finished the final session with a clear mandate for participants. He asked them to do two things, which we subsequently codified and tracked in some detail. The first was to share the experience and learning with their own teams, so that the time away was better understood as a learning programme (which others might want to join in the future). The second was to write back to him within two weeks with specific actions showing how the learning could be turned into tangible opportunities to better engage with clients.

China itself provided a clear opportunity to engage with clients who either knew the market and region well, or had no exposure or interest to date in the region beyond Hong Kong and Singapore. The obsessive customer focus found at Alibaba and in meeting other business executives prompted debate about how the organisation could better partner with the local branch and institutional business in China, better access local knowledge, improve access to services and products, and help navigate complex regulatory and cultural differences. Meares closed the week by challenging the group to think about ways in which the firm could use some of the lessons learned on culture, galvanising employees around ambitious, stretching goals. How could the HPDP group in an established large international business instill something of the zip and energy of the "start-up" spirit felt in Hangzhou?

Two years later, 49 of the 50 participants from the HPDP cohort who visited China were still with the business. This may not sound remarkable, but in a hot market for talent with mobility, ambition and rare skills, retention was a great outcome for the business. The cost of the programme was a significant investment, but was a mere "rounding error" compared to the opportunity cost of hiring and retaining a group of people this good.

Meares worked hard to develop a relationship with the cohort members, and he encouraged members of his executive team to do the same. The cohort had developed a connection with one another that had a significant impact for many of them and for their subsequent lives and careers. Many talked about the greater sense of ownership they felt for their work and a sense of belonging in the firm.

Meares made a habit of calling on various members of the cohort for special projects to ask them to attend client marketing events. He asked a sub-group to help organise the firm's annual strategy workshop, to take part in regional marketing initiatives and to lead a new product development function. When travelling into local markets for Board or customer meetings, he would often call on members of the HPDP for a coffee and a chat. He made sure someone from the smaller international offices stayed plugged into the group head-office initiatives. He got to know the cohort members well, their names, their families, listening to their grumbles about the firm, as well as their new ideas. The annual compensation process was adjusted so the Senior Management team could monitor the progression, or otherwise, of members of the cohort. When the business in the UK ran the due diligence on a major acquisition target, many of those in the confidential deal room had been on the China visit two years earlier.

Meares deliberately built a network across the business that was less intensely involved in boardroom debates and politics, yet who intimately knew the business, its customers and how change initiatives might land, or not, with employees. He built on Bannister's approach, actively connecting talented managers around the world. By extending this approach beyond new hire induction into a well-regarded learning and development programme, with the explicit goal of better serving the needs of clients, he was continuously creating collaborative networks that he could access. By tapping into the HPDP cohort for support, ideas and feedback, he was deepening his own relationships and encouraging the participants to do the same. He might not have described it as such, but he was cultivating a powerful kind of glue.

All good things must . . .

Like all the best business stories, there is, of course, a sting in the tale.

Meares was replaced as CEO of the business in 2012, and his successor, Krishna Patel, an investment banker, had none of Meares' instincts for talent development. While Meares departed to become Chairman of Quilter, Patel wasted little time to make his mark, shifting the organisational focus to one of retrenchment and cost control, with a management style marked by rigorous performance management and scrutinising expenses. One of his early decisions was to mothball the HPDP programme, as well as global induction, and he introduced a more centralised management model led out of Switzerland. This approach, combined with the imposition of strict regulatory oversight and compliance requirements, meant a major change in outlook for the business. The HSBC Group seemed poised to sell, or close, much of its private banking business and many of its best talent started to leave the bank.

The halcyon days of the business and an investment in glue were clearly over.

Reflections

It is easy to make value judgements about these leadership decisions. Of course, no one instinctively applauds the leader who cuts the training and induction budget. It was, though, no big deal for Patel. Bannister and Meares were enlightened, positive investors in talent, whom we might admire. Patel took a different view and thought he would get alignment through a bigger emphasis on renumeration, and that connecting with other parts of the HSBC Group was more important than building relationships within the private bank itself. However we perceive their different approaches, they each made and owned very distinct choices about people, talent, organisational development and how best to serve clients.

Patel's approach was not unusual amongst corporate senior executives: focused on the bottom line, emphasising performance management and strong control from the centre. With hindsight, the leadership approach of Bannister and Meares, who were seasoned, experienced managers, seemed in many ways distinctive, enlightened and unusual. Surprisingly, their approach also echoed something of the Jack Ma story. While Ma was a mercurial innovator, from a different sector and different part of the world, all three leaders were simply trying to find good ways to fire up, motivate, engage and get the best from a small group of talented colleagues.

Those shared leadership behaviours are worth considering. They each sought to galvanise a talented group of individuals around an ambitious goal: requiring total commitment, long hours and high-performance; investing their own personal time and energy; encouraging collaboration, insight and learning. They were obsessed with improving things for customers and ensured other members of their leadership team had the same priorities. They were personally visible, highly accessible, taking time to listen, as well as communicating clearly. For them, it was important that everyone involved felt that they would share in the rewards created, and they looked for ways to help others to see the world differently.

You may find nothing extraordinary or particularly mind-blowing about these behaviours, but in my experience, at the top of many corporations, they are rare and unusual. In combination, the results created were compelling: motivating talent, retaining their interest and creating a dynamic amongst the group that better served customers. As I came across other role-model leaders through learning events, and leadership workshops, the behaviours were consistent and familiar: galvanising talent, setting ambitious goals, being accessible, investing time, listening, engaging deeply, connecting across teams, making customers the focus . . . each an essential ingredient of glue.

Ten years later

A decade later, I met up with one of the cohort members, now a Partner in a venture capital firm.

She had stayed with the HSBC Group for a few years after 2010, and was promoted, leading several corporate development activities for the business. She was still in touch with many of the cohort, and because of the deep connections she had made, had felt more confident a few years later to leave the bank in the UK and take up an offer to work in Asia. She described her participation in the HPDP programme as one of the most valuable things she had done in her career.

Applying glue

- When was last time a learning programme, or other experience at work, gave you an "aha" moment?
- What did you do with that insight? Who did you share it with? If not then, why not do it now?
- What specifically did Jack Ma do to **galvanise** the team? What would that look like in your firm?

Notes and references

1 Expo 2010, officially the "Expo 2010 Shanghai China", was held on both banks of the Huangpu River in Shanghai, China, from 1 May to 31 October 2010.
2 Jack Ma arranged for his speech in the flat to be video-recorded. Transcript is from YouTube. https://youtu.be/Up9-C4_8dVo
3 Yifan Xie, Stella. 10 September 2018. Barron's online article. "Jack Ma Is Stepping Down at Alibaba. He Was a Showman Who Showed China a New Way to Do Business." https://www.barrons.com/articles/jack-ma-leaving-alibaba-1536594946
4 Clark, D. (2016) *Alibaba: The House That Jack Ma Built*. Ecco. Excellent account of the rise of Alibaba, China's momentous economic and social change, and the company's charismatic founder Jack Ma.
5 Clark, D. (2016) Ibid., p. 36.

3

THE ADVANTAGE OF GLUE

With so many workers now "scrolling alone", firms that create
and nurture glue give themselves an organisational advantage.

The post-programme learning review with the China cohort was one of the
best moments of my career, with the participants each sharing a real sense
that the learning experience was both powerfully felt and immediately
applicable. Having spent a week immersed together, the cohort wanted to
keep in touch, work with one another again, stay connected, and not just
within the context of the HPDP, but on China-related projects, common
problems within the business and future opportunities to work again with
the CEO. One of the cohort members described her experience "as the
single best week of my career at HSBC", and she was not alone in enthusing
about the learning experience and the closeness found amongst colleagues.

On the plane home from China, I had been listening to "Star Guitar"
by The Chemical Brothers.[1] The music was not my usual headphone filler,
but the tune coincided with a rare moment of lucidity on my part, and the

DOI: 10.4324/9781003410690-4

middle-section refrain in the song took on more meaning than it ought. If you have not heard it, "Star Guitar" is a great dance track which cleverly contains a four-bar acoustic guitar sample from the beginning of David Bowie's song "Starman", hence the name, "Star Guitar". This sample is repeated throughout the track, with various musical elements building and morphing as it progresses. The only lyrical element is a sample refrain: "You should feel what I feel, you should take what I take."

Describing now, some years later, a rare moment of insight, 30,000 feet in the air, flying over Russia, with the Chemical Brothers' paean to drug-fuelled euphoria on repeat, probably makes little sense when written down here in a business book. But at the time, I was like Archimedes emerging from the bathtub, enlightened and energised.

Maybe glue was a kind of benign workplace drug? The ultimate performance stimulant? A consistent theme connecting disparate parts? Some secret sauce in the organisational mix?

Tired, I had probably overdone the metaphors by that stage, but the glue idea lasted long beyond landing, immigration, customs, a return home and then back to the office. There had been many insights on that trip (forgive me) and the aftereffects were long-lasting. This idea of glue certainly felt worth exploring further, and it has since formed a touchstone for just about every learning experience I have been involved in. Over a decade later those moments of discovery and the "aha" experience in Hangzhou are still fondly felt.

After the programme in China, I took some time to reflect on the various insights and the early ideas about "how to nurture glue" were beginning to form. I talked about it a lot with the HPDP cohort and others, exploring their experience and the value they found from close collaboration with others they would not normally connect with day to day. In the subsequent years, I have worked closely with the senior teams within dozens of different organisations in Europe, Asia and the US, and have been fortunate to work on programmes with very many executives from some of the largest companies in the world.

But not all these experiences have been like those with the HPDP group, or its sponsors.

Sadly, that epiphany sensed in China was quickly found to be even more precious and rare. Of the many organisations that I have worked with since, glue, if found at all, was awfully scarce.

A world without glue

Working life is not always a bed of roses. Some organisations are powered by very different forces than glue, where managers are obsessed with status and hierarchy, while employees, over-burdened with bureaucracy, are "motivated" by opaque reward mechanisms, not their leaders. Senior managers must arm wrestle with corporate cultures of "up-or-out" or "fit-in-or-f-off" and they become fixated on "survive to fifty-five", threatened by force-ranked performance management processes, led by charismatic but unapproachable executives. I regret that many of my colleagues had moments in their careers marked by episodes of bullying and fear.

Thankfully, most of the senior leaders I have personally worked for have been supportive, challenging and encouraging. A few demonstrated these qualities and more, often exhibited all at once. Unfortunately, one or two have been veritable psychopaths, including one senior executive who would fire contract staff while bouncing a tennis ball off the wall above their heads as the boom-box under his desk blasted out "Another One Bites the Dust".[2]

I will spare their blushes, but these experiences have been with firms that appeared outwardly successful, profitable, well-known brands and highly regarded employers. But despite their reputations, very few of their senior leaders ever expressed any great love for their firm, one another, their leaders or their customers.

Undeterred, I never stopped looking for glue, and then I would talk excitedly, with little coherence, to my colleagues whenever and wherever some was discovered. I have found that the organisations with glue were easier to navigate, more fun to work with and more difficult to leave. Glue added to the experience as an employee, and when I worked with new firms whilst engaged as a consultant, glue was one of the first things I went looking for. It felt important to find.

I began to codify some of that learning from "glue-rich" environments and those leaders who cultivated glue. I then drafted some definitions for a better understanding of the phenomenon, researched some related management theory and developed some ideas for action that leaders could adopt. There was, in that research, the need to find some solid anchors of belief, and I was fortunate to meet, hear and learn from some inspirational management thinkers, as well as observe the role-model behaviours of some unusual leaders. Before we get to a narrower definition of what I mean by glue, let me share some of that research and those anchors of belief.

The right environment for glue

You might naturally think of glue as being about encouraging collaboration, or engagement or stronger internal relationships. Some leaders might talk about glue in other ways, describing the value of their organisation's "unique culture", their "brand essence", the "firm's DNA" or "the way things are done around here". All these ways of describing the organisation are right to consider, though it often seems hard to clarify what they mean exactly, and the behaviours that they entail are difficult to codify. But in the very specific way I have seen glue demonstrated, there is something more profound happening and, crucially, something that can help join different parts of the organisation together, so they are not just examples of productive teamwork within established intact teams.

The essence of glue is not fluffy and amorphous, but visible and action oriented. That tangibility is found in what your best people do and are seen to be doing. In particular, it is not just about their individual contribution, which may be enormously valuable, but also their propensity to connect. The essence of glue is found in the strength and connectivity of relationships amongst your most valuable people and the value that creates. But for something to happen, it needs the right environment and context for those collaborative behaviours to emerge.

When we enter any organisation, we cannot help but notice the subliminal signals of atmosphere, mood and tone, which we quickly absorb. These are clues to the typical behavioural context in which the firms' employees either survive, or hopefully, thrive. In a book by the late Professor Sumantra Ghoshal,[3] he memorably described this environment as either feeling like the "energy sapping environment of downtime Calcutta in mid-summer, or the Fontainebleau Forest in spring".[4] If the culture of the organisation feels oppressive, compliance heavy and personally stifling, "it saps all the initiative, creativity and commitment from their people".[5] Ghoshal argues that if the environment feels like downtown Calcutta, you cannot make employees give more of themselves (for example, being more creative or entrepreneurial) simply by sending them on a training course or attempting to change their "mindset".

The onus is on an organisation's leaders to actively create the right environment for people's entrepreneurship, creativity and collaboration to flourish. In my experience, Ghoshal captured it perfectly. Creating the right environment for glue is not done by memo, or corporate video or an internal "values" campaign; it is done by leaders adopting and exhibiting the right behaviours and role-modelling ways of working that emphasise the value found in others.

Social capital

It might be helpful if we dig a little deeper into management theory and add some substance to these claims about organisations, and why encouraging collaboration is a noble pursuit, but also an uphill task, as described by the sociologist Pierre Bourdieu:[6]

> The existence of connections is not a natural given, or even a social given . . . it is the product of an endless effort at institutions.[7]

With glue, I am not talking about some hocus-pocus or "voodoo" theory of leadership and organisations. There is, in fact, a long heritage of academic research around an important and closely related concept called "social capital" which underpins our search for glue. Social capital is a way of describing the internal social and cultural coherence of society and, because of this, social capital has been described as a kind of glue.[8]

Social capital is not as well-known as some other popular management theories, like behavioural science (sometimes referred to as "nudge" theory), influence (particularly work by Robert B. Cialdini, the American psychologist), situational leadership or psychological safety. An article by Sumantra Ghoshal and his co-author Janine Nahapiet neatly describes the concept of social capital and its origins:

> The term "social capital" first appeared in community studies, highlighting the central importance for the survival, and functioning of city neighbourhoods, of the networks of strong, crosscutting personal relationships developed over time that provide the basis for trust, cooperation, and collective action in such communities. Early usage also indicated the significance of social capital for the individual: the set of resources inherent in family relations and in community social

organisations . . . researchers increasingly have focused their attention on the role of social capital as an influence not only on the development of human capital, but on the economic performance of firms.[9]

High levels of social capital are associated with a number of positive societal benefits including social trust, engaged citizenship and strong reciprocity, without which communities would not function so effectively. For individuals, social capital is regarded as important because it is an "important source of power and influence that helps people to 'get by' and 'get ahead'".[10] There are many interesting studies of "social capital" which look closely at the societal, or community, context – including *Bowling Alone: The Collapse and Revival of American Community* by Robert D. Putnam, a breakthrough book published in 2000. Putnam succinctly defines social capital as:

> The connections among individuals' social networks and the norms of reciprocity and trustworthiness that arise from them.[11]

Using a wide variety of data sources, Putnam shows how Americans have become increasingly disconnected from one another. His book paints a stark picture of rapidly declining social capital in the USA from the 1960s to the turn of the 20th century. He describes Americans' changing behaviours, with "bowling alone" (rather than in groups as part of after-work clubs) used as a metaphor for a society that is becoming increasingly disconnected from one another with less involvement in their local parent–teacher associations, churches and political parties, and he describes the harm that these broken bonds create in society.

Putnam's central argument in his book is that both civic engagement and organisational involvement saw marked declines in the latter part of the 20th century. Fewer and fewer Americans are socialising through membership organisations, with churches, political parties, volunteer organisations and trade unions all seeing a collapse in numbers. Putnam's book (and the article on which it was based a few years earlier) created a huge stir in academia, and Putnam found himself in "the middle of a deluge of discussion, debate, and dissent around the questions it provoked".[12] His central thesis was not a happy one, with America pictured as place of increasing dislocation and a sense of decline of the American dream itself.

Putnam was overwhelmed by the response to his book, along with the tide of feeling, further research and debate it generated. In a revised edition, published 20 years after the original, he includes some thoughts on the impact of the internet and social media, but even in his original book from 2000, he writes about the effect of a different kind of addictive screen that became inculcated into our homes and lives: the television set.

> Time diaries show that husbands and wives spend three or four times as much watching television together as they spend talking to each other and six to seven times as much as they spend on community activities outside the home. Moreover, as the number of TV sets per household multiplies, even watching together becomes rarer. At least half of all American usually watch by themselves.[13]

As the title of his book suggests, Putnam does not end the original book on a gloomy note, and makes the case for revival, through learning from the past – referring to the beginning of the 20th century, when dramatic technological, economic and social change rendered obsolete a significant stock of social capital due to industrial revolution, rapid urbanisation and new immigration. In response to this, Putnam comments that the leaders of the day re-developed social capital with an "extraordinary burst of social inventiveness and political reform",[14] and he notes the substantial increases in the standard of living and the founding, or refurbishing, of many contemporary civic institutions such as the Boy Scouts movement or the National Association for the Advancement of Colored People (NAACP).

While Putnam admits that the specific reforms of the past might not be appropriate for the present, he makes a number of suggestions to revive social capital which, along with some ideas about education, political decentralisation and religion, include "more family-oriented workplaces, which allow for the formation of social capital on the job" and "technologies that reinforce, rather than replace, face-to-face interaction should be encouraged".[15] Three decades after his original research, you can make your own assessment of how successful society, in the US and elsewhere, has been in achieving these two aims since Putnam published his book.

In the 2020 revised edition, he helpfully revisits some of the other ways in which Americans have become more connected than ever, and become visibly re-engaged in local issues and politics through the medium of the internet and social media. He seems, though, unconvinced that the explosion of Facebook, Instagram, Twitter and other social media platforms has replaced the value of personal social interaction. The ubiquity of smart phones and the addictive lure of social media and tailored feeds have connected us deeply into an alternative digital world, but have personally disconnected us from one another:

> People are often physically together in a collective space at a breakfast table, in a business meeting, even sitting at a bar – engaged not with others who are present but with a cell phone, surfing the Web. They are alone together. We seem to be communicating more but listening less.[16]

While Putnam is exploring social capital in a community context, the same concept translates well to business organisations, where in an increasingly disconnected, remote and "hybrid" working world, the social bonds are, if not broken, certainly loosened or more intermittent. I mentioned earlier that organisations are experiencing a growing sense of disassociation, between employee and employer, as well as, and more worryingly, between employee and employee. Organisations are starting to take this seriously, including technology companies who, unabashed, are at the forefront of encouraging remote and hybrid working. A major study by Microsoft on the effects of remote work on collaboration amongst information workers was published in *Nature Human Behaviour* in September 2021. The study compared information workers' behaviours before the Covid-19 pandemic and then after the introduction of mandatory home working in March 2020. The conclusions were not good:

> Overall, we found that the shift to remote work caused the formal business groups and informal communities within Microsoft to become less interconnected and more siloed. Remote work caused the share of collaboration time employees spent with cross-group connections to drop by about 25% of the pre-pandemic level. Furthermore, firm-wide remote work caused separate groups to become more intraconnected by adding more connections within themselves. The shift to remote work also caused the organisational structure at Microsoft to become less dynamic; Microsoft employees added fewer new collaborators and shed fewer existing ones.[17]

Another survey at the same company in 2022 looked at manager and employee perceptions of homeworking, which continued long after the pandemic-related restrictions were lifted. Surveying 20,000 people across 11 countries, Microsoft found that employers and employees fundamentally disagreed about productivity: 87% of employees felt that they worked as, or more, efficiently from home, but only one-fifth of the managers agreed.[18]

It seems that in the rush to empty offices and work from our homes, we may have moved to a different kind of disconnect, from "bowling alone" to "scrolling alone".

The organisational advantage

The most useful and pertinent explanation of the importance of social capital, in a business context, is one proposed by Sumantra Ghoshal, which he terms "the organisational advantage".[19] His research hypothesises that a "firm's ability to create and utilise social capital contributes to performance differences among firms".[20] One of the reasons for this advantage is that strong social capital, through exchange and collaboration, aids the creation of intellectual capital, which adds value to the firm.

Citing numerous sources, Ghoshal's theory even offers a clear-cut business case for that much-debated issue within firms: whether to spend money on internal events and social gatherings. Ahead of planning your next workplace party, you may wish to forward Ghoshal's cogent argument to your finance department.

> These can be viewed as collective investment strategies for the institutional creation and maintenance of dense networks of social relationships and for the resources embedded within, available through, and derived from such networks of relationships. Alternatively, these meetings and social events provide the unplanned and unstructured opportunities for the accidental coming together of ideas that may lead to the serendipitous development of new intellectual capital.[21]

But these social relationships, these connections and collaborations, are not a free-for-all knees-up for all-comers. Ghoshal's research points towards the key contributing factors that create value. He shows that new intellectual capital is not just borne out of a random process of bringing people together, but importantly: "Those firms developing particular configurations of social capital are likely to be more successful."[22]

He suggests three key dimensions to that configuration. These need to be networks that can be readily **accessed**, and the participants need to **anticipate** that there is value to be created by connecting and be **motivated** to do so.

Ghoshal adds to this something called "combination capability", creating the right network environment for collaboration and ideas exchange. Firms that get this configuration of circumstance and motives right generate new intellectual capital (new ideas, initiatives and opportunities), as well as improved relationships, higher levels of trust and stronger bonds amongst the group. He notes some limitations, as there is obviously a cost to doing these things well, and if the behavioural norms of the connected group are not right, it might have a negative consequence. On balance, he advocates the benefits of investment in actively nurturing social capital, to create good outcomes for the firm. Where firms do this well, this can give them an organisational advantage.

> We suggest that differences between firms, including differences in performance, may represent differences in their ability to create and exploit social capital. Moreover, at least regarding the development of intellectual capital, those firms developing particular configurations of social capital are likely to be more successful. Evidence for this suggestion is found in studies of knowledge-intensive firms that have been shown to invest heavily in resources, including physical facilities, to encourage the development of strong personal and team relationships, high levels of personal trust, norm-based control, and strong connections across porous boundaries.[23]

In summary, Ghoshal argues that social capital, properly harnessed, can create more intellectual capital, which can provide an **organisational advantage** to the firm. There is a business case, a commercial imperative even, to ensuring that firms invest in approaches and people strategies that encourage more social capital.

For our purposes here (see Figure 3.1), Ghoshal's theory has been adapted to reflect some of the specific dynamics observed within in glue-creating firms. In particular, the increased incidence of experiments and creativity seen in firms with vibrant internal cultures, where diverse talent is connected and stretched. The model illustrated is not static. Each of the three dimensions needs to be continually refreshed. The impetus comes from the creation of social capital, which strengthens interpersonal relationships, evidenced by better connected employees, more exchange and more collaboration. This builds valuable friendships, reciprocity and trust. This, in turn, contributes to the creation of more intellectual capital, which builds new knowledge, ideas and innovation. This can lead to better employee engagement, customer focus and, in time, improvements in productivity and growth. External talent is likely to be attracted to firms perceived to have this "organisational advantage", adding to, and refreshing, the pool of resources cultivating social capital.

The beneficial cycle makes sense, but it makes even more profound sense if you take away social capital as one of the three elements. The firm without social capital will exhaust itself on old ideas and be held back

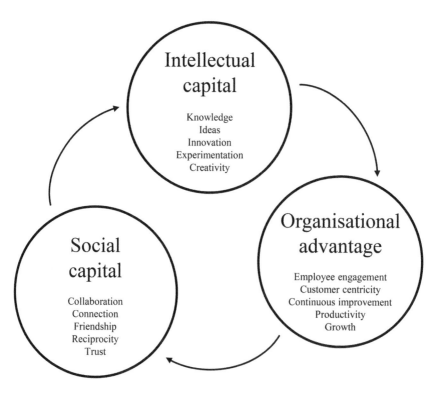

Figure 3.1 Model based on Sumantra Ghoshal's "organisational advantage"[24]

by a lack of innovation and experimentation. Ultimately, this will further deteriorate engagement, productivity and slow growth. This is the great risk of the hybrid age – of disengagement and diminished collaborative intent leading to declining social capital, thus denuding firms of the very energy and vitality we know creates innovation and ultimately advantage for the firm. It is why this book opened with the prime importance leaders should give to the creation of glue.

A key concern for us is to work out how social capital can be productively nurtured and, in our organisations, how our talented people are best configured to create that value. I suggest some practical "configurations" (either through creating talent cohorts or using business experiments) in Chapters 5 and 7. For now, though, it is worth emphasising that this organisational advantage will not just happen naturally or through serendipity. In an increasingly remote, or hybrid, working world, business leaders need to work even harder to encourage these productive connections. We cannot rely on the hybrid firm to generate social capital without intervention. As Bourdieu said, it will only happen in your organisation as "the product of an endless effort".

Some recommended research and resources about social capital, including Putnam, Bourdieu, Ghoshal and others, are included in the Resources section at the end of this book. It is deep work of a particular kind to enter the realm of these intellectual giants and their research but, like any investment in learning, it is gold dust once discovered. My intention here is mainly to provide some of the thinking about the social capital foundations on which we can encourage and nurture glue.

Applying glue

- Would you say social capital is abundant in your firm or in decline?
- Has hybrid working helped or hindered this?
- What do you or others in your firm already do to increase social interaction, connection and networking amongst colleagues?
- How could this be made more deliberate or purposeful (for example, specific opportunities to connect colleagues from different part of the organisation)?

Notes and references

1   The Chemical Brothers are a British electronic music duo composed of Tom Rowlands and Ed Simons. Originating in Manchester in 1991 they were pioneers in bringing the big beat genre to the forefront of pop culture. The song "Star Guitar" is from the album *Come With Us*, released in 2002.

2   "Another One Bites the Dust" is a song by the British rock band Queen. The song was featured on the group's eighth studio album *The Game* released in 1980.

3   Sumantra Ghoshal (1948–2004). Ghoshal was an Indian-born scholar and educator who worked as a Professor of Strategic and International Management at London Business School and was the founding Dean of the Indian School of Business in Hyderabad, India. His book *Managing Across Borders: The Transnational Solution* (2002), published by Random House and co-authored with Christopher Bartlett, has been listed in the *Financial Times* as one of the 50 most influential management books.

4   Ghoshal, S. and Bartlett, C.A. (2000) *The Individualised Corporation: A Fundamentally New Approach to Management*. Random House, p. 142. The book is particularly relevant to our considerations here about organisations and culture, presenting a fundamentally new view of management, emphasising that human creativity and individual initiative are the most important source of competitive advantage.

5   Ghoshal, S. and Bartlett, C.A. (2000) ibid., p. 142.

6   Pierre Bourdieu (1930–2002) was a French sociologist and public intellectual, primarily associated with the School for Advanced Studies in the Social Sciences in Paris, and the Collège de France. He was one of the first scholars to use the term "social-capital".

7   Bourdieu, P. Richardson, J. (1986) *The Forms of Capital: Handbook of Theory and Research for the Sociology of Education*. Westport, pp. 241–258.

8   Claridge T. (7 December 2014) "Introduction to Social Capital." Retrieved from: https://www.socialcapitalresearch.com/why-is-social-capital-so-important/

9   Ghoshal, A. and Nahapiet, J. (April 1998) "Social Capital, Intellectual Capital, and the Organizational Advantage." *The Academy of Management Review*, Vol. 23, No. 2, pp. 242–266. Notes: Comprehensive explanation of the concept of social-capital, taken further, explored, and applied. Abstract: "Scholars of the theory of the firm have begun to emphasise the sources and conditions of what has been described as 'the organizational advantage,' rather than focus on the causes and consequences of market failure. Typically, researchers see such organizational advantage as accruing from the particular capabilities organisations have for creating and sharing knowledge. In this article we seek to contribute to this body of work by

developing the following arguments: (1) social capital facilitates the creation of new intellectual capital; (2) organizations, as institutional settings, are conducive to the development of high levels of social capital; and (3) it is because of their more dense social capital that firms, within certain limits, have an advantage over markets in creating and sharing intellectual capital. We present a model that incorporates this overall argument in the form of a series of hypothesized relationships between different dimensions of social capital and the main mechanisms and processes necessary for the creation of intellectual capital."

10 Claridge T. (7 December 2014) op. cit.

11 Putnam, Robert P. (2000) *Bowling Alone: The Collapse and Revival of American Community.* Simon & Schuster, p. 11. The book was developed from his 1995 essay entitled "Bowling Alone: America's Declining Social Capital", an essay on civic disengagement in the United States published in *Journal of Democracy* 6 January 1995: pp. 65–78. According to one commentator, it is "perhaps the most discussed social science article of the twentieth century".

12 Preface to the 20th Anniversary edition, Putnam (2000) ibid., p. 1.

13 Ibid., p. 224.

14 Ibid., p. 368.

15 Summary of Putnam's proposals for revival of social capital from an article by Brett Reeder, "Conflict Research Consortium". Retrieved from: https://www.beyondintractability.org/bksum/putnam-bowling.

16 Afterword to the 20th anniversary edition, Putnam, Robert P. (2020) *Bowling Alone: The Collapse and Revival of American Community*, Simon & Schuster, pp. 424–425.

17 Yang, L., Holtz, D., Jaffe, S. et al. (2022) "The Effects of Remote Work on Collaboration Among Information Workers." *Nature Human Behaviour*, 6, pp. 43–54. https://doi.org/10.1038/s41562-021-01196-4

18 Sourced from: https://news.microsoft.com/2022/09/22/microsoft-unveils-new-research-and-technology-to-bridge-the-disconnect-between-leaders-and-employees-so-companies-can-thrive-amid-economic-uncertainty/

19 Ghoshal, Sumantra and Nahapiet, Janine. Op. cit. "Social Capital, Intellectual Capital, and the Organizational Advantage." April 1998. The *Academy of Management Review*, Vol. 23, No. 2, pp. 242–266.

20 Ibid.

21 Ibid.

22 Ibid.

23 Ibid.

24 See Ghoshal, Sumantra, and Nahapiet, Janine. "Social Capital, Intellectual Capital, and the Organizational Advantage." April 1998. *The Academy of Management Review*, Vol. 23, No. 2.

4

DEFINING GLUE

The cultivation of glue should be your principal leadership concern.

We have looked at the importance of glue, sharing some sense of its impact, reflecting on the China experience, as well as some observations about other places and firms. If the underpinning management theory that improving social-capital creates an "organisational advantage" is correct, then there is a genuine imperative for firms to invest in activities and people strategies that cultivate glue. But encouraging and maintaining social capital amongst every single employee is rarely possible. Therefore, an investment in glue should be carefully considered and clearly focused.

But what does this glue look like and where is it most evident? More pertinently, if you wanted to explain this idea of glue to a colleague, or you wanted start to look for glue your firm, how might you describe it?

DOI: 10.4324/9781003410690-5

Certainly, there are characteristics of exhibited behaviours that make glue distinctive amongst particular groupings of your people. In the Introduction a rather wordy definition was offered:

A powerful dynamic of highly engaged talented people serving one another, the organisation, and their customers, enabling the organisation to grow and thrive.

As a shorter edit, glue will be referred to throughout this book, as more simply:

The powerful dynamic of highly engaged talented people, enabling the organisation to grow and thrive.

Simplification of the definition does not mean it's party time, where the only thing you need to look out for is smartly dressed types high-fiving, drinking the coolade, and watching the share price soar. I will spend time later digging into the vital relational dimensions of "one another", the "organisation" and "customers" because the reason the enterprise grows and thrives is because of the strength of connectivity of these three partners in the relationship.

So welcome to the glue-rich firm, where there is a tangible sense of the powerful dynamic of highly engaged talented people, enabling the organisation to grow and thrive. It sounds simple, but in my experience, it is indubitably rare. As such, it is hugely valuable.

Searching for glue

Think about your own organisation. Look around. How much glue do you see? Glue might not be immediately obvious as you scan your organisation because it is, by its nature, somewhat hard to discern. It only becomes apparent through very closely observing the collaborative behaviours, actions and outlook of your organisation's very best people.

As such (and here is the real magic), it can be spotted, as well as encouraged and nurtured. Be assured, some glue is already there in your organisation, though you may have to search around to find it. But once you discover glue and start to harness its power, the effect can be revolutionary. You cannot help but be amazed by its effect. But you can be driven to distraction when you find that it is absent.

Your principal leadership concern

Given that the societal forces and trends suggest employee engagement is worsening, and the full potential amongst your best people is probably not fully tapped, the upside of working to create glue ought to be a priority. Moreover, as we saw in Chapter 3, Ghoshal and others have shown that there is a distinct organisational advantage to be found in the very act of trying. The cultivation of social capital, an essential ingredient of glue, should be your principal leadership concern.

Even if you make it an absolute priority, glue will not appear overnight. It needs three crucial things to happen:

1. **It requires careful identification of your most valuable people.**

   The careful identification of your most valuable people should be seen and felt to be a profound, meaningful exercise, not a cursory paper-review of likely successors and high-performers. Too often, these talent processes are just that: processes. Often the process is diarised like an audit, delegated like an unloved responsibility, and outsourced to smart-suited outsiders whose general model for spotting talent is well meant but, ultimately, is not truly owned by you. Like any rare and precious asset, you need to look hard, explore alternative routes, and dig deep to find your most valuable people. The search for talent needs to be a collaborative responsibility of the firm's top team and, ideally, the CEO should be seen to own that search personally.

2. **It demands your deep personal engagement with your most valuable people.**

   This can be time-consuming, at times troubling and somewhat uncomfortable. No one else can do it though. If it is not part of your personal mission to be amidst and embroiled in nurturing glue, then the likelihood is that no one else will make it happen. In a glue rich environment, your senior leaders will personally know your most valuable people and find imaginative ways to get them to combine well, serving one another, the firm and your customers.

3. **It needs you to create and mandate strategically important, innovation-led opportunities, for your most valuable people.**

These strategically important innovation projects, or business "experiments", and their outcomes, are things you must care about as much as the day-to-day stewardship of strategy, business planning and good governance. If you are pursuing a new strategy, or managing change, glue can make things more cohesive. But cultivation is not some strange remote osmosis, for example, asking selected teams to simply "greenhouse" some new ideas, and see what they come up with. It needs resources, planning, structure, scheduled inputs and senior leaders' active, personal and visible involvement.

In summary, Figure 4.1 gives the "PowerPoint bullets" version of what is required to start creating glue (and it really is this simple):

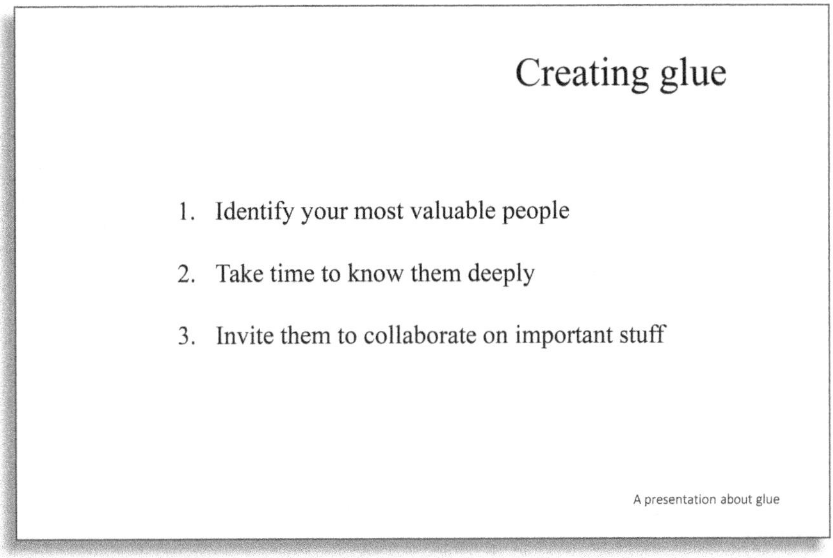

Creating glue

1. Identify your most valuable people

2. Take time to know them deeply

3. Invite them to collaborate on important stuff

A presentation about glue

Figure 4.1 PowerPoint slide version of how to start creating glue

You may well be wondering if it is that easy, why bother with the rest of the book? You could, of course, save the time, rally round some smart people, buy them lunch, ask them to share a few stories and then give them an important project to wrestle with. Job done?

Unfortunately, each of these relatively simple things listed 1–3 can be fiendishly difficult to actually make happen. Activation can be problematic, and the leadership behaviours needed are seldom ingrained into the way an organisation already works. Take, for example, task 1 – the simple task of identifying your most valuable people (Figure 4.1). (Later in this chapter, we will cover tasks 2 and 3 – taking time to know them deeply; and inviting them to collaborate on important stuff.)

Task 1: Identify your most valuable people

Glue requires the careful identification of your most valuable people (see Figure 4.1 earlier).

The point is so important I will offer it again:

Identifying your most valuable people is crucial to creating glue.

But what do you look for? In seeking to find top performers, their skills and attributes will be wide-ranging. In identifying talent, those who enjoy innovation and change may well be important to you. Those with technical, data analytical and digital skills may be highly valued, as will those who show creativity, drive, energy, ethics, values and a whole range of other qualities. There will be many role types, functions and departments to be included in your search. The HPDP cohort mentioned in Chapter 2 was made up of more than 20 different roles from back-office, head office and relationship management teams.

Importantly, you also need to find those who have a deep understanding of your customers, regardless of their function, location or seniority. The approach of those organisations who have "back to the floor" exercises for senior executives, or who second head-office and technical staff into stores, contact centres and client-facing roles, makes much sense.

When Tesco in the UK hire executives from outside into the business, they often insist that the shortlisted candidates spend a day shadowing a store manager in one of their flagship stores. There they discover the employee mood, the customer experience and the problems at "the coal face". But why not do this the other way round? Ensure that your corporate learning and development programmes, which typically favour the strategic, finance and managerial types, bring those who know your customers best more closely into the fold.

Stars that align

Glue is about carefully and deliberately identifying, inspiring, empowering and unleashing small cohorts of talent.

Focusing on a small but diverse cohort of powerfully motivated talented people is more likely to be impactful than broad brush people-policy making or other tactical interventions, such as firm-wide training, standardised induction and employee-engagement surveys. This is not the meaningless force-ranking of the top 20% of "high" performers, distinct from the 70% of "median" performers and 10% of "under-performers". You do not need to benchmark your employee engagement scores against the global Gallup norms[1] to already know that your highly engaged already represent a pitifully small percentage of your overall staff. Many HR-led employee engagement programmes quickly become diluted in an attempt to embrace the many.

You do not need to shy away from making genuine investment to encourage, enable and develop "stars" in your organisation, but your approach should not be designed to make them stars alone, but stars that align.

At the outset this search for "most valuable" people can seem like searching for needles amongst various haystacks. The best people to help you drive change are distributed across different departments, locations, functions and are at different stages of their careers. The usual route of spotting talent across hierarchy and grade levels can often only identify a thin slice of talent, at the same age and stage, rather than help you aggregate the very best resources from across the firm.

Identifying great individuals to compile a talent list is not on its own enough. In a glue-rich organisation it is about visibly supporting and recognising the way that talented individuals form relationships that serve one another. Those with an ability to connect and collaborate are key to the whole venture.

The criteria for identifying talent should emphasise what that person has positively done for their clients, for the organisation or for their colleagues, not what grade-related succession process or future "competency" model they might fit. You cannot rely on outdated two-dimensional balanced scorecards or nine-box grids, or place too much value on organisation charts and psychometric tools. There are organisational psychologists, and talent advisors who can design and run a process of assessment and benchmarking of your top performers. The crucial difference is not the rigour of their process, but your own personal involvement and ownership of the outcomes. Glue comes first from a committed senior leadership, very often characterised through the personal commitment and conviction of the CEO and their attitude towards talent.

There is nothing new in identifying and nurturing cohorts of talented people, and "your most valuable people" is a deliberately broad description for a cohort that you hope will become a hot bed of glue. Your best people can evidence future potential, rare talent, key skills, and scarce capability, but they are not necessarily going to be the "usual suspects" already familiar to the senior leadership team. And, even with the best, most specific competence and behavioural science-based evaluation criteria for "most valuable people", you will also run into some hairy problems.

- **Your most valuable people are probably already heading for the door**. Those with the most ambition and curiosity are those most likely to leave by being directly poached, headhunted or through simply being bored. Rather than fester as a "quiet quitter", they are likely to leave the mature enterprise for the "start-up" route because they have the energy, ideas and entrepreneurial gas to burn. Jack Ma made every one of his founder group shareholders from day one, including his driver. What is the equivalent signal or approach that you are using to retain your best people?
- **Your most valuable people are likely to be difficult to manage**. In their book Clever,[2] Rob Goffee and Gareth Jones, both Professors at London Business School, describe such talented types as "Clevers", those super-smart employees who create the most value for organisations, but also need careful, attentive management so that their talents and potential can be best realised. They look closely at talent within the technology, engineering, consulting and creative industries. The smartest, most creative people in these organisations might elsewhere be described as geeks, mavericks and loners. Goffee and Jones say that they provide a

unique leadership challenge because the relationship with your most talented individuals is not the same as other employees.

> Leading clevers is hard. Remember there is a paradox at work here. Clevers challenge several aspects of the traditional working relationship. First, they don't want to be led, but they need leadership to achieve their potential and create value. Second, they enjoy a symbiotic relationship with the organisation. In the past, individuals were expected to add value to the organisation, but in the clever economy, the organisation and its leaders must ask themselves, how they can add value to their clever individuals.[3]

- For the organisation to get the best value out of these super-smart employees, it is important that they are closely connected with others who are similarly blessed. You have to convince them of the value of "the team" through creating shared goals, interdependence, and awareness of one another. Goffee and Jones suggest that this best happens through serendipity, that your most talented people will somehow discover one another. In a hybrid working world this serendipity is less likely than ever. My view is that connecting these "clevers" is too precious an opportunity to be left to happenstance. Leaders need to engineer and design smart ways to get top talent to coalesce, connect and collaborate. If talent is both distributed widely (different departments and functions) and remote working, so physically distanced from one another, the action of bringing them together in person in cohort groups for development, experiments or as a forum for you to listen, can be hugely impactful. But to do that it takes huge effort on your part – devising the forum, engaging with the individuals closely and creating stimulating challenges for them to collaborate on. This can be time consuming and exhausting, or else, see the point about exits earlier.

- **Your most valuable people are unlikely to be in your head office.** Don Sul, with Rebecca Homkes and Charles Sul, identified a different cohort of important talent in a major study of effective strategy execution.[4] They highlighted key "distributed leaders" and managers who have been around for many years, or are relatively new, but who deeply understand the organisation, its dynamics and "how to get things done". As the name suggests "distributed" means they could be literally anywhere and at any level with the organisation, so the thoroughness of your talent search is key. In leading change, Sul and his colleagues demonstrate the importance of coordinating across silos, not just communicating from the top down. The breadth as well as the depth of your talent search is important. As with the consequences of managing that talent pool, it needs time and energy to ensure that you find and embrace these distributed leaders, and to connect with the super-smart contributors.

- **Crucially, your most valuable people will not necessarily look like you**. Not only will they often look different to you and to one another, as a cohort, they will not all be the same age or be at the same stage of their careers. You need to cast your net wide and often, look hard and explore the organisation purposefully to uncover the most talented people for your glue-rich cohort.

Glue includes, not excludes

This repeated emphasis on your organisation's "best people" or "most valuable people" is sensitive territory in which to tread, without easily sounding old-fashioned, elitist or worse.

It seems increasingly unfashionable to focus on "star performers" and, given much recent historical corporate malfeasance, it is not a territory to wade into lightly. Inherent in the definition of "most valuable people" is a process of selectivity, with the obvious danger of falling into the traps of unconscious bias, exclusion or discrimination. It is vital that your search for talent works hand in hand with your inclusive people strategies and, where deeper consideration and advice is needed, that you closely involve diversity, equity and inclusion expertise to ensure your talent cohorts are not just a coalition of the "usual suspects". That should not mean senior leaders do not take the personal lead in identifying and nurturing talent, just that they should do it using expertise that ensures inclusion, not exclusion.

You should also seek diverse contributions about talent from across the whole organisation. The occupants of the executive suite are unlikely to be the sole arbiters of good sense in an organisation. A good way of doing this is to identify those "distributed leaders" who deeply understand the organisation and its dynamics. They may not be from top universities or high-fliers from the graduate scheme. They may not be from a privileged or wealthy socio-economic group. They may not have done an MBA, or worked in your firm's most successful offices, or high-profile departments. They may have worked for the organisation for 30 years, not five. When you work with them, they may not see the world as you do, but do not balk at sourcing diverse perspectives that are not normally heard, as well as those that are contrarian and counter intuitive.

The great value of difference

Solving the thorny dilemmas that arise in pursuing a new strategy, executing a plan, or leading change tend not to be epoch-making binary decisions, but finer margin calls that require careful judgement. They rely helpfully on gut feeling, but also on good data, critical evaluation, impartial advice and a practiced wariness of the "bias" traps of confirmation, escalation and commitment. Most of all, decisions are best not taken in an echo chamber of nodding assent, but by involving diverse colleagues who feel able to challenge the way you see the world.

The best results arise from teams that harness a mix of skills and a diversity of minds, perspective and backgrounds. This is a broad assertion and difficult to prove across the panoply of decisions in complex organisations. Also, of course, leaders can vary and improve their decision-making approach with experience. But you can use small experiments to illustrate problem-solving failings using business games, simulations and management tests. A favourite of mine is a well-worn test we use with senior audiences in our Executive Education Programmes at London Business School.

We ask cohorts to work in competitive teams, each challenged to replicate exactly a fabricated product, against the clock. The twist is that only one member of each team, at any one time, can actually see what the original product looks like. Good dialogue, consensus and collaboration then become key. As the deadline approaches, smart decisions about the build process, materials, colours, form and dimensions become increasingly crucial. Some teams fail the task, give up or query the process and available resources. But we also clearly see and unpack some useful learning from those teams who are successful.

The heroes in the exercise are seldom those who charge ahead with a bullish strategy, executed at speed. Often those teams miss the vital clues around them and the alternative solutions, particularly those within their own team. We observe that the best performing teams have leaders who keep the tempo high, but also pause, listen and check with others. It may be surprising to hear that often the quietest, least assertive team members (who perhaps have a better sense of design and the creation process) are often the ones who shine. The team leaders who actively consult and listen most carefully, are often the ones who win.

When you think about talent bringing diversity and difference, do not be surprised if the way you think about the boundaries of your search ends up being much broader than you first thought. If you want difference and diversity in your collaborative cohorts, you should also not be bound by the context, location and dominant culture of where your employees work. Harper Reed is a tech entrepreneur and was Chief Technology Officer for Barack Obama's 2012 re-election campaign.[5] He says that we should radically stretch our thinking about how we go about putting together diverse teams in a digital world.

> Products are now for the internet and the internet is a hyper-diverse place. And if you don't have a team that represents the internet's diversity, then your products aren't going to be any good.[6]

As you consider your pool or talent, seek diverse ideas, generationally. You may already have ways to encourage your new graduate recruits, or other employee groups, to share their ideas. Many organisations now have "Next Generation Boards" to bring a different perspective to the leadership team. Perhaps members of those forums could help create glue, not just be a sounding board?

Task 2: Take time to know them deeply

Glue demands your deep personal engagement with your most valuable people. As Figure 4.1 earlier suggests, the task here is to take time to know those people deeply.

I have had the privilege of working with senior executive leaders, successful entrepreneurs and high-value clients. Many of these business leaders have inspired, intrigued and terrified me in equal measure. Quite rightly, in dozens of business books and management journals, the leadership journey of successful CEOs is often the focus. You only have to spend a brief time with the CEO of a major organisation to understand what it takes to lead a substantial enterprise. It's obviously hard work. It's often painful, sacrificial, exhausting and unforgiving. It's tough at the top. Worse still, it's often lonely. For the ones I have met, the route to senior leadership was evident in the tough calls they had made about their lifestyle and the depth of their commitment to their organisations. It was also easy to spot some of the mental and physical scars of leadership, which became more obvious as the years went by and the turbulent markets, long hours and stress took their toll.

The irony then is that I am strongly advocating that the time-pressed, stressed-out senior executive invests more, not less, time in their organisation.

You need to find ways to reduce or subtract other activities to dedicate time to glue.

The very best leaders I have seen did something even more remarkable than simply thrive and survive the machinations and travails of life at the top. They could clearly manage and communicate effectively to run the business. As I looked closer, the best leaders were also able to deepen their engagement and relationships not just with their senior "top-team" people, but crucially, with and between their most valuable people. They created glue.

Leaders can set their tone, not just through their own personal interest in their best people, but also through signalling that their expectation should be the norm.

To illustrate, I vividly remember one experience, early in my career, working in the head office of Barclays in the UK. I joined a meeting with the newly appointed Group Chief Operating Officer (COO) and the Head of Public Relations to talk about a recent corporate acquisition and what would mean for the incoming senior executives who would be joining as part of the deal. Some would be announced as direct reports to the CEO; others were in regulated roles, where formal announcement would be required; yet others would be leaving the business post-completion of the deal.

I knew the Head of PR by name, but I did not know her very well, beyond having met her across the table in previous formal meetings. When the Group COO asked about our working together before, I remember his face dropping, realising that we were not already as thick as thieves. The Group COO expected his senior people to be well acquainted and close, not just connected by the happenstance of a meeting or a deal. He wanted alignment, and to be able to call upon managers who could immediately "click" and get things done. Maybe he asked, or assumed, too much in the busy hubbub of a head office of numerous departments, silos and fiefdoms? But his visible disappointment at the absence of glue stuck with me.

A suspension of disbelief

The best leaders not only understand the idea of glue, but they also make good use of it. They have the ability to extend their influence beyond the core strategic role of steering the executive team, communicating upwards to the Board and managing external shareholders and stakeholders.

Critically, they are also able to engage the hearts and minds of talented people widely distributed across the organisation, often in far-flung territories and seldom visited markets.

These leaders are able to engender something special amongst their most valuable people. Duncan Clark talks about Steve Jobs' "reality distortion filed" as something Jack Ma tried to emulate.[7] I prefer to describe it in the way filmmakers talk about creating a "suspension of disbelief".

These leaders created an absence, or at least a dramatically lower level, of cynicism amongst cohorts of very diverse and talented people.

Despite the vagaries and often vacuous nature of corporate life, their contributions felt markedly more meaningful. The corporate "bullshit" quotient seemed significantly lower when very senior executives made sincere and generous contributions of time and energy to engagement, rather than distant and remote, communicating via channels and head office missives.

In a way, this rare "suspension of disbelief" is at the heart of this book and the very nature of glue. One way these leaders reduced the cynicism was to make the focus "outside" the organisation, not the preoccupation and politics of inside. The "secret sauce" was often the emphasis on the external customer as the focus of the firm's endeavours; a shared purpose that felt important and meaningful. They helped people to look at the organisation from the "outside in".

In this way, the very best leaders are able to use glue to create powerful relationships between particular people, not just within the firm but with customers and clients as well. They aim to make customers the key beneficiaries of glue. These deeper relationships with customers are not a product of clever brand marketing, or personal glad-handing by the senior leader, but are maintained through harnessing the best possible collaboration of the most valuable people within the organisation.

These beneficial relationships can be transformed into improved client loyalty, increased referrals and more recommendations. For example, in one major wealth management firm I worked with found that presenting the firm's offer to clients through joined-up collaborative teams from the same talent group (but from very different parts of the firm), created a significant rise in key client engagement and the realisable benefits of increased loyalty and advocacy from those clients. The management team could demonstrate real improvement, with engagement scores tracked and measured quantitatively and qualitatively.

In a highly competitive market, where clients are often served by multiple firms, these engagement scores matter enormously. The leaders of the wealth-management firm who invested in glue (through their talent cohort) remarked on two things achieved at once: the organisation was a place where colleagues engaged more effectively internally with one another; and they also engaged better with the firm's clients. Internal glue became external glue.

Task 3: Invite them to collaborate

Referring back to Figure 4.1, the final task in creating glue is to invite your most valuable people to collaborate on important stuff.

Glue needs you to create and mandate strategically important, innovation-led opportunities for your most valuable people. Encouraging glue can serve the organisation well but connecting the super-smart talents and the execution experts distributed around the firm will not happen organically. The glue needs to be carefully engendered amongst both groups, and, in a particular way.

What is key is how these diverse performers are knitted together, challenged, and engaged to support one another across the organisation. This "harnessing" is vital and should be a proactive role of the CEO and senior leadership team. At its best, these high performers are encouraged to try out ideas on creative, imaginative innovation projects. Often these are best set up as fail-fast business experiments that are designed to illuminate truths about products or strategy ideas or customer needs.

These collaboration opportunities are more valuable than a promotion to ever-deeper in-trays, more bureaucracy, greater spans of control and fancier job titles. High performing individuals don't just need to oversee and control broad competencies; they also need to be let off the leash. In Chapters 7 and 8, we will look much more closely at how providing autonomy and freedom to experiment can be a powerful way of motivating and energising talent and thereby creating glue.

Harnessing glue can be used as a lever for organisational development. If you free up leadership airtime and subtract many peripheral activities and initiatives, leaders can have more scope to address thorny organisational problems. If leaders have the time to invest themselves in glue, rather than other broad-brush corporate and inward facing corporate initiatives, the evidence is that much can be achieved, including experiments that create new products, grow revenues, and improve the bottom line. But glue also helps address organisational development itself; breaking down silos, creating cross-functional connections, improving communication and client insight, deploying diverse perspectives to common problems, onboarding new hires and integrating talent secured, for example, following a merger or acquisition.

Making it happen

In summary, creating and nurturing a powerful dynamic of highly engaged talented people should be your principal leadership concern. As we have seen throughout this chapter, and as listed in Figure 4.1, there are three critical ways to do this: carefully identify talent; get to know those with talent well; and connect them through strategically important initiatives.

It is simple in concept, but in execution it can prove to be difficult because talent is hard to find, keep and engage, and your own time is scarce, making it a challenge to get to know those with talent well. One of the best ways to do this is to get your most valuable people to coalesce around solving thorny business problems. Find opportunities for them to collaborate, using business experiments, or other initiatives, to create better outcomes for customers.

You will send a bold leadership signal through the way you prioritise your own time and energy into sponsoring these initiatives, investing in these individuals, and making it clear that those outcomes are important to you and to the organisation. In doing so, you can create a suspension of disbelief through your visible personal engagement and openness, making their contributions feel more meaningful.

The reality is this is not something that magically happens with a wand, a re-jig of the diary and a few well-chosen people and projects. It needs a significant re-adjustment of focus across the year and requires new leadership behaviours and habits. You also need to be determined to subtract, freeing up time for this different kind of focus. Whatever your approach to creating glue, your success will not be determined by what you decide to do, but the way you go about it.

Over the next few chapters, we will look at different ways in which you might build relationships across and down the organisation, and role model that as the leadership norm.

You can also view glue creation as an exercise in organisational development, using key moments across the year for communication, planning, workshops and leadership forums as opportunities to engender and harness glue. Business experiments are enormously valuable, and we will look in more detail at how these can be set up for success, both as collaboration opportunities and also to create great outcomes for the business.

So, before I look more closely at what you might do, let us look at some of the leadership behaviours exemplified in creating glue.

Applying glue

- What do you think about the definition of glue? Where and when have you seen this dynamic appear in your firm?
- How deeply and how often do you and your firm's leadership team talk about talent?
- In what ways and by which criteria would you determine "your most valuable people"?

- How broad, deep and wide is your pool of talent, and have you ensured diversity in all senses?
- What could you do (subtract) to find more time for glue?

Notes and references

1 Gallop provides a whole range of reports and services to measure and benchmark employee engagement at: https://advise.gallup.com/employee-engagement, and https://www.gallup.com/

2 Goffee, R. and Jones, G. (2009) *Clever: Leading Your Smartest Most Creative People*. Harvard Business Press.

3 Ibid., p. 64.

4 Sull, D., Homkes, R. and Sull, C. (March 2015) "Why Strategy Execution Unravels – and What to Do About It". *Harvard Business Review*, Vol. 93, No. 3, pp. 58–66.

5 You can find out more about this "awesome" (his word) individual at www.harperreed.com

6 This quote is from a lecture by Harper Reed in 2016, given at the an open lecture series in London called the Braintree talks.

7 Clark, D. (2016) *Alibaba: The House That Jack Ma Built*. Ecco, p. 25.

5

LEADING WITH GLUE

Leading with glue requires an investment in relationships across
and down through the organisation. You need to listen, engage
and galvanise others, often in unusual ways.

The opening premise of this book was that leadership is not just about you;
it is about them.

For many, that new emphasis is an awkward shift from the mode normally
encouraged by coaching, peer advice and study, which often focuses on
a better understanding of self, and adjustments in personal approach,
mindset and habits, rather than a new obsession with the competence and
engagement of your team members and their colleagues.

Given that you are up for the challenge, how do you make a change
of emphasis clearly visible to others in the organisation and what might
you personally do to make that recognised? Like many other aspects of
organisational change, it starts and ends with the type of exhibited
leadership behaviours that are observed, recognised and emulated in the

DOI: 10.4324/9781003410690-6

firm. There are dozens that might help to make a notable shift, though four seem to be pivotal in moving from managing, to leading with glue.

Which leadership behaviours are required?

Leading with glue is typified by four complementary qualities: an ability to **galvanise**, actively **listen**, be **unusual**, and to **engage** others (see Figure 5.1).

There is no happenstance in the construction of this "glue" mnemonic; it's an obvious acronym that hopefully sticks in the mind! There are, of course, numerous other qualities constantly demanded of the modern leader, but, these are the ones that best serve your principal goal to be an active creator of glue – and you start by galvanising a group people.

Galvanising

You need to be able to galvanise – i.e. "to excite others about something, so that action is taken".[1] That is task number 1.

There are very many occasions in working life when a leader's ability to galvanise is essential. You are a film or theatre director, with a new

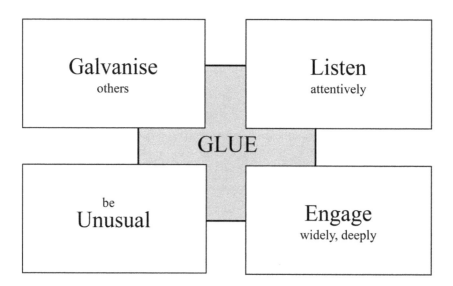

Figure 5.1 Four key leadership behaviours for leading with glue

production and a rapidly approaching date for the curtain to rise. You are a product manager, reluctant to ship something that is not perfect, but your competitors appear ready to steal your thunder and you need to get the engineers to make major changes quickly. You lead compliance and risk management for a major information services provider and need to overhaul security before the regulator imposes crippling requirements. You need to work with your CFO, bankers and lawyers to close the deal before the target acquisition is lost to another acquirer.

Being able to act quickly with agility and confidence in those circumstances is a critical and rare leadership skill. But being able to do that and then respond and execute by harnessing others, from different departments, or geographies, or disciplines or with different degrees of confidence in the plan, is an even rarer level of accomplishment. Being able to do that – to galvanise others – when the pressure and complexity gauges are all turned up to 11 is an extraordinarily valuable leadership skill.

The leader who can excite others about the future, winning hearts and minds, and draw the best from all involved at critical moments, is right to be applauded and feted. The glue-minded leader does this, not by relying on their own capabilities but by making sure they already know the skills and abilities that they can draw upon. They do not wait for the moment of crisis, or sudden opportunity, to reach out broadly for support; they have spent time engaging widely, connecting the dots, identifying talent, searching for rare skills and encouraging collaborative behaviours. They see these moments as opportunities to unleash the talent of others.

In developing your ability to galvanise, your task is not to get the whole organisation on board. We need to be realistic; no one person can do that, no matter how much charisma, energy and resources they throw at the task. Too many company development initiatives are like mass "sheep dip" exercises: vast and pan-galactic in scope, too broad and woolly in their goals and, as they extend over months and years, energy, attention and impact wane. Instead, your focus is a talented few, preferably from different, disparate parts of the organisation. Your goal is more immediate and focused: to ignite the imagination of a talented cohort and excite them about the role they can play, now and in the future.

An insanely great example

The archetypal "galvanise" story is Steve Jobs' creation and launch of the Macintosh computer in 1984. It is a well-known story, but the hero of the tale is often Jobs himself, the visionary genius, a maverick, who had "insanely great" ideas, facing off against the gigantic competitor IBM and their game changing product, the PC. There is, of course, much of Jobs' personality in the tale and millions of words have been written exploring the good and bad of Jobs' leadership style. The more pertinent story is the extraordinary quality of the team he created, and how he galvanised a small group of talented engineers, designers and product specialists to change the personal computer forever.

In 1982 Jobs was ostensibly Chairman of Apple Inc., a company employing 6,000 people, but when he took control of the Macintosh project, he reverted to "start-up" mode and as hands-on project leader. He raided talent from within Apple, and recruited, persuaded and gathered staff from different parts of Apple to bring together a cohort of talents. Amongst them were John Raskin (the originator of the Macintosh project), Brian Howard, Joanna Hoffman, Burrell Smith, Bud Tribble, Bob Belleville, Steve Capps, George Crow, Donn Denman, Chris Espinosa, Andy Hertzfeld, Bruce Horn, Susan Kare, Larry Kenyon and Caroline Rose. Raskin departed abruptly when Jobs took firm reins on the project, but many stayed and in 1984 a core team of 48 were credited with the design and launch of the first Mac.[2]

These were heady days at Apple, with its mercurial founder dedicating most of his time to the Mac team, leading a project in direct competition with another Apple team creating the higher-specification Lisa computer. With Raskin removed, Jobs set about creating an exceptional "task force", poaching engineers from other projects and visibly signalling both personal ownership and corporate separation of the taskforce. He moved the Mac team to different offices, spending a million US dollars on a new building known as Bandley Three. One of the team, Steve Capps, flew a pirate Jolly Roger flag above the building. Jobs' biographers Brent Schlender and Rick Tetzeli describe Jobs as behaving like he was "back in the garage" where he had founded Apple with Steve Wozniak eight years earlier, "rallying the gang, leading and inspiring a small team of extremely creative people".[3]

Jobs drove the team ferociously, with team members working through public holidays and some forgetting their own birthdays. When there was a break, Jobs took the group offsite on retreats, using his skills as an inspirational speaker to implore them to stick with the project, despite problems and delays. Schlender and Tetzeli describe the intensity of Jobs' grip on the team, but also the depth of collaboration and commitment he created amongst the group. While some quit, exhausted and broken by the relentlessness, others were enthralled:

> [They were a] small group of folks who loved it so much they stuck around, ready to do whatever it would take to do it all again, in order to work in the rarefied, exhilarating charged atmosphere that Jobs created.[4]

If you were lucky enough to own an original Macintosh, and if you went to the effort of dismantling the exterior, inside you would find the Macintosh teams' signatures engraved in the plastic of the original Macintosh case. The idea (according to Jobs) was that since the original Macintosh was art and artists sign their work, the original Macintosh team should sign theirs. So, they did. The signatures are inside the case, seen by very few people . . . but they are there. Andy Hertzfeld, a member of the original team describes the story this way:

> First and foremost, Steve Jobs thought of himself as an artist, and he encouraged the design team to think of ourselves that way, too. Since the Macintosh team were artists, it was only appropriate that we sign our work. Steve came up with the awesome idea of having each team member's signature engraved on the hard tool that moulded the plastic case, so our signatures would appear inside the case of every Mac that rolled off the production line. We held a special signing party after one of our weekly meetings. Steve gave a little speech about artists signing their work, and then cake and champagne were served as he called each team member to step forward and sign their name for posterity.[5]

The nature and depth of collaboration that Jobs created is hard to appreciate from a distance, but luckily there was a short and wonderfully insightful film produced at the time. *In Search Of Excellence*, a documentary produced by John Nathan, based on Tom Peters' bestselling business book,[6] profiled six excellent companies.[7] The segment about Apple Computer was filmed in the summer of 1984, featuring interviews with Steve Jobs and the original Macintosh team, and opens with footage of the Jolly Roger pirate flag waving in the wind. The insights are incredible, with some terrific moments from Jobs, orally eviscerating his behemoth competitor IBM. But, appropriately, it is the small team that he put together that is the main focus. The narrator captures the mood:

> Jobs wanted the new task force to behave like pirates, outside corporate law. He was determined that this team would be free to innovate unencumbered by Apple's bureaucracy and he led the project himself. Jobs was a perfect model of the new manager as coach, cheerleader and nourisher of champions.[8]

For balance, one of the team members, Chris Espinosa, describes Jobs as a "maniac" and an obsessive control freak, but others explain that they needed the air cover he provided to do their best work. Burrell Smith, a hardware expert, described that rarity of environment: "Steve Jobs was a catalyst for us; he gave us space, he sheltered us from the corporate noise."[9]

And Jobs enthused about the tightness of the group, focused on a common goal.

> The neatest thing that happens is when you get a core group of, you know, ten great people, that it becomes self-policing as to who they let into that group.[10]

For the documentary makers, the Macintosh team demonstrated how effectively a task force can innovate when it is bound together by a shared vision and given the freedom within the corporation to find its own way. A software engineer, Rony Rebok, describes the common motivation:

> Everybody just wanted to work, not because it was work that had to be done, but it was because something that we really believed in that was gonna really make a difference.[11]

The other fascinating aspect of the story is that this small group galvanised by Jobs was not made up of seasoned managerial types who had been around for years, but those with "technology at the tips of their fingers and in their passion, the latest understanding of where technology was and what we could do with that technology".[12] The captions in the documentary tell you the rest:

> Steve Jobs, age 28 years, Chairman; Chris Espinosa, age 23, Manager, User Education; Burrell Smith, age 28, Hardware Wizard; Andy Hertzfeld, age 30, Software Engineer; Rony Rebok, age 23, Software Engineer; Joanna Hoffman, age 29, Marketing Manager; Bud Tribble, age 31, Software manager.[13]

From top to bottom, this was an incredibly young team, unencumbered by cynicism and fuelled by shared ambition.

If you roll the Apple story through the next decade, there was much turmoil and change, as Jobs left the company he founded, leading different ventures including NeXT and Pixar, and then there was a form of redemption when Jobs returned to Apple in 1996. The rest is, as they say, history with Jobs subsequently launching the iPhone and a suite of sought-after products and service innovations, becoming one of the most valuable enterprises in the world.[14] Tellingly, Jobs was interviewed in 2010 and asked again about how he got the best out of people:

> We are (still) organised like a start-up. There's tremendous teamwork at the top of the company which filters down to tremendous teamwork throughout the company . . . and teamwork is dependent on trusting the other folks to come through with their part without watching them through with their parts, and that's what we do really well.[15]

Jobs' explanation was not about his own attributes as leader, but one about the value of collaboration and trust in the business. Key ingredients of glue.

Elon Musk needed all vectors to align

The Steve Jobs story has been deconstructed and revisited often since his death, with the darker side of his ego, his fearsome nature, bullying, coldness and control-freakery becoming the preferred focus of biographers and film-makers. I still have a poster on the wall (next to his rather curt email to me) which celebrates the "crazy ones, the misfits, the rebels, and the trouble-makers".[16] It seems with great talent comes great foibility.

In more recent years, the poster boy mega-entrepreneur has become Elon Musk. Despite his astonishing achievements at PayPal, Tesla, SpaceX and Starlink, he is not everyone's favourite multi-billionaire. He has his quirks, unfiltered Twitter addiction, punchy views and an interest in everything from controversial neuralink technology, artificial intelligence and crypto currency. He clearly is a man of incalculable genius and entrepreneurial vision – an exceptional human being with rare behaviours and yet, some strange emotional vacuity.

To become the richest man on the planet (notably, from a standing start) has needed an unfathomable work ethic and a profound sense of the future, a vision for a more sustainable planet and the opportunity for human exploration beyond this earth. He also realised in building SpaceX and Tesla that he could not do it alone. Like Jobs, he set out to "acquire" the very best talent he could, for example hiring George Blankenship, who created the global Apple Stores, to design and run the new salesroom stores for Tesla. When he needed to galvanise and lead others, he adopted a team philosophy that is Steve Jobs-like in its brevity and acuity.

Thomas Mueller is a Rocket Propulsion Engineer at SpaceX and was "employee number 1" when hired by Musk. He talks of Musk's determination to get the whole team wholly focused and completely committed to the success of the venture. After an early rocket exploded on an island in the Pacific, Musk exited some engineers and others he felt were not fully committed. Mueller describes Musk's approach like this:

> I noticed that if people were negative, they were not in the next meeting. He said a company is a bunch of vectors, each person is a vector, and they need to point in the direction you want to go. Bureaucracy and office politics and low morale, it's almost random vectors. He was always about making all the vectors, which are all the employees, pointing in the right direction forward, always moving forward.[17]

Launching a rocket into space and then smoothly landing it the right way up on a small barge out at sea obviously requires all the science, engineering and software to be perfectly in sync. This needs discipline, accuracy, quality control, testing and re-testing. To launch and land re-usable rockets, Musk needed all people to similarly align. If you see films of the Mission Control rooms of the NASA Apollo moon landings, or the Space Shuttle missions, you will see rows of men huddled over terminals, and a disembodied voice announcing the flight status, with call signs and succinct technical updates.

When you see the control room of SpaceX, with its enormous glass wall, you will see hundreds of employees packed together tracking the mission status in nano-second real-time on their phones and iPads. When a rocket successfully lands on one of Musk's quirkily named floating barges, it is like the crowd scenes following a winning touchdown in a US college football championship game. A riot of young people, hugging and screaming and shouting and embracing the sheer life-affirming joy of that achievement, together.[18] I often wonder what would it be like to work for a firm where success is felt so powerfully and celebrated like that. How is the equivalent success celebrated in your firm, and can they hear you yelling from down the street?

Listening

The fashionable mode of the modern senior leader is to be highly visible. Many CEOs will carefully and systematically carve out time in their schedules to be out and about in the business, appearing as part of a familiar suite of interventions, presenting, glad-handing, cutting ribbons, chairing meetings, fronting town halls and roadshows covering the latest results or strategic update. This is all well meant, but is seldom effective in growing engagement, and almost certainly a peripheral activity, if the real objective is to create glue. The magic leadership mode, and the key differentiator needed, is not the impact of visibility in "broadcast" mode, but in taking the time to listen.

If you are the CEO, or part of the senior leadership team of your firm, then you are expected to set the vision, communicate that clearly and, when asked, have thoughtful clear answers. But your leadership super-power is probably much more rarely used: the application of your listening skills.

Jeremy Darroch hears some feedback

Jeremy Darroch, the former CEO and Executive Chairman of Sky, ran the business for 14 years, before managing the sale of Sky to Comcast, the American media and communications giant, in 2018 for £30 billion. This made Sky the most valuable UK company to be sold in the last 30 years. Darroch's tenure at Sky saw its growth and transformation into Europe's largest and most valuable multi-platform media company, serving over 23 million households throughout Europe. Sky became a major creative and innovative force in the media industry globally and, as Darroch executed a series of successful merger and acquisition programmes, it also became one of the largest investors in the European content industries and a major creative force across Europe.

Like other glue creating leaders, Darroch put great emphasis on creating the right working environment to encourage collaboration and innovation, re-building Sky's headquarter campus in West London and Sky Studios Elstree into state-of-the-art working facilities and exemplars of modern-day, environmentally responsible, working practices. As a leader he exudes authenticity: proud of his heritage and education in the North-East of England, understated and unfussy in his manner, but full of acuity, with an ability to process, explain and make sense of complexity and explain strategy with real clarity.

Darroch tells a compelling story about the importance of listening. It was a moment of listening that changed the way he and his team talked about the business. He describes his preferred leadership mode as "management by walking around" and using that time to listen and better understand what is happening in the business. On one visit to Sky's customer contact centre in Scotland, Darroch met one of the contact staff, whom he had met before and whose views he enjoyed hearing. She was helpfully direct: "Jeremy," she asked, "why are you never happy?" He was taken back by her question. She went on to explain that so much was negative around the business, unsettled by change initiative after change initiative – it felt like change for change's sake, and it was distracting and tiresome.

Sky's motto was "Believe in better", and while that provided a promise to customers and a compelling stretch for its business ambition, Darroch said that it also became "a rod for our own back" with some managers tackling too many initiatives, or seeking to resolve internal gripes, under the cover of serving the firm's promise. The reality was that the business had got much inherently right, including the improvement in the quality of its customer contact centres, and exceptional levels of customer-led ideas and innovative new products. But change was being used as a blunt tool and so Darroch began (with his management team) to talk less about change and more about "renewal". The semantic change seems minor but, for Darroch, his employee's feedback highlighted the importance, as the business matured, of using the right words. For some employees the need for change suggested rejection, while "renewal" meant that many existing approaches could be continued, made better and improved.[19]

Leaders can quickly and helpfully amplify their listening skills. At town halls, or in meetings with colleagues, listen carefully to the question, pause and then answer the question. It sounds simple, but it needs a particular effort and approach to do this well. Another true story might illustrate how this can go horribly wrong and on an enormous scale.

The importance of being seen to listen

I worked for an organisation which had just promoted a new global CEO. On appointment, he embarked upon an ambitious global roadshow of live set-piece presentations around the world. The endeavour was to cover the majority of the business operations in about three weeks, with the CEO using a private jet to hop from country to country, hosting a series of town-hall meetings, presenting to tens of thousands of managers on every continent. This was, by any measure, a huge logistical and physical undertaking. He would speak at separate events in Switzerland, Germany, Scotland and London during the same day, before crossing the Atlantic and covering the US in several stops, without a break, then continuing, via dozens of stop-offs, covering Bermuda, Latin America and the US, then back across to the Middle East, India, China, South-East Asia and Australia.

All employees could track his progress online on an interactive global map, which showed the status of his journey and where he would literally take off and land. His communication team hired an expensive professional events agency, which seamlessly made each venue he presented in look like the last. The format of each event was the same: a serious strategy presentation and then an opportunity for mangers to ask questions. The CEO's communications teams and advisors seemingly voiced no particular concerns about the optics of the global roadshow, even though his predecessor had done much to improve the business' sustainability credentials in the previous years.

The CEO's ambition for the business was immense and his hefty PowerPoint deck was lengthy, dense with data, rich with ideas, intensely rehearsed and he was ready to go. But the issue was not the roadshow, nor the ridiculousness of how it all sounds today in an environment of more considered largesse, zoom calls and more sophisticated styles of messaging. The problem was not even his presentation style, which although lacking warmth showed him to be demonstrably open and visible – prepared to communicate in great detail about what needed to happen to reshape the business. As he strode onto the stage, with pulsating music and lights, the accompanying motivational video faded to black and the spotlight was fixed on him. This was an executive at the top of his game, in charge of his brief and ready to execute his ambitious agenda. The problem emerged when the presentation finished, and he stayed on stage for the Q & A.

He was very sharp. He knew the business, the markets, the regulatory environment and the competitor landscape. We were packed in to hear him at the Odeon Theatre, Leicester Square (London), a cavernous place that normally showed blockbusters like a Star Wars or James Bond movie rather than a CEO roadshow. As the CEO finished his presentation, a large microphone boom was extended over our heads from the aisles. A regional manager asked a straightforward question about investment in systems, which had been neglected for years. The CEO answered him immediately, authoritatively and brusquely, and then asked for another question, like a boxer ready for the next punch. Another brave soul asked about hiring, and he instantaneously nailed the issue, said what needed to be done and what he would do in response. The room became unsettled, and murmurs and grumbles began to sound in the hall. Another question, another immediate and authoritative answer. Another question and, bang, his answer flooring any risk of any doubt.

There was nothing particularly wrong with the answers, or even the monotony of such indefatigability exuded from the stage. The problem was that the CEO never paused before answering – not even for a second. Despite the vast expense on venue, impressive staging and top-end event production, the overwhelming impression left was of a CEO who preferred to be the expert, to not particularly care who had asked the question or how deep the issue was felt, but who wanted to be seen as the only person the room who could solve it.

I do not know if there was ever a full debrief with his communications team evaluating the impact of the roadshow, or whether they felt he had captured any more hearts and minds. But as we shuffled out of the theatre, blinking into the light, there was a palpable sense of disappointment. It was not because he did not have something interesting to say, but that he did not even take a second to listen, acknowledge a question well made, or ask for clarification. He just answered. One of the most expensive and ambitious internal communications campaigns in corporate history may have served only to make the CEO seem more remote, not less.

Insight and application

It is a tiny detail in the great panoply of things leaders need to think about: but, if someone asks you a question – particularly in a public forum – always acknowledge the questioner, pause . . . and ensure that you have heard, or understood, it correctly. Then be thoughtful and considered in your response. Otherwise, no matter how succinct and apposite your answer, you run the risk of looking like the only thing you care about is the answer, not the question, nor the questioner. In that moment of pause, you will let others sense you actually having listened.

There is strong evidence that listening is a leadership super-power. Carl Rogers, in a classic 1952 *Harvard Business Review* paper,[20] theorised that when speakers feel that listeners are being empathic, attentive and non-judgemental, they relax and more readily share their inner feelings and thoughts without worrying about what listeners will think of them. This safe state enables speakers to delve deeper into their consciousness and discover new insights about themselves, even those who may challenge previously held beliefs and perceptions. If you want to get to know more about people, at a deeper level, it seems asking fewer questions and simply listening more enables that.

Perhaps because listening, as a leadership behaviour, seems somewhat passive, it is undervalued? Another listening story might help further illustrate the point.

How are you?

In 2006 I worked closely with a highly dynamic CEO, who had many laudable qualities and was in many ways an exemplar creator of glue. However, like all of us, he had his own blind spots. One incident was hugely memorable and important, when he inadvertently shared out loud his own "failure to listen" story.

I had hired a group of professional actors called Steps[21] to help the organisation better understand issues of diversity and inclusion. Steps had been formed in 1992, while role-playing for the student doctors at Guy's Hospital Medical School (London). In fact, they used to meet on the steps of the school, which gave them their unusual name. They are now an international and successful learning business that creates dramatic learning programmes grounded in, and reflective of, organisational reality. In writing and playing out dramatic scenarios to which executives have to respond and react, they literally "hold a mirror up to the world" and this can be a powerful way to help individuals to recognise their own and others' behaviours.

For the firm, Steps ran a series of scenarios where the audience was engaged in watching a catastrophic mess of bad behaviours, clumsy language, insensitivity and unconscious bias. The afternoon was well run, but it was the Steps lead facilitator's debrief that created the biggest learning point, and notably it was the most senior executive in the room who shared it.

The CEO explained that he would visit the firm's many international offices and would aim to be as visible and accessible as he could. When he worked out of the firm's London office, he avoided the closed meetings rooms and deliberately booked a glass-fronted spare office, on the busiest floor, where all staff could see that he was there and, if they wanted, could pop in and speak to him. Few did, but his offer was well known. In the afternoons, he would walk the floors, saying hello to as many employees as he could, as he briskly navigated the building.

Over time he got to meet more and more familiar faces and, even if less familiar, he would always say; "Oh hello again, how are you?" In the workshop debrief, the facilitator from Steps asked him to pause, and play back that phrase to the whole audience. He looked uncomfortable and repeated it, "Oh hello, how are you?" The CEO was very sharp, and he knew where this line of enquiry was going. So, in front of 50 senior colleagues, he opened up and shared the truth honestly: "I say 'Hello, how are you?', and I just say it . . . it seems the right thing to say, but I don't really mean it." It was quite an admission, but he shared it with the whole management team.

When asked, he explained that employees would say "Fine", and he would move on, but he quietly lived in fear that someone would say, "Well actually, I'm not great, and the reason is this . . .". His approach was intended to signal him being friendly, open and accessible, but he was not really inviting openness, just being platitudinal and moving on.

I am not sure if the CEO in any way adjusted his approach thereafter, taking more time to pause and listen, but the very fact that he opened up and admitted he was just skimming past people, not really enquiring into how they felt, was quite an extraordinary thing to admit in front of a large group of leaders. I believe that he did not lose any respect for being authentically open about his closed behaviour.

The need for acuity

Listening is not just about being sound of hearing. There is an even rarer super-power, and a form of listening, observing and thinking combined. Only the very best leaders demonstrate something called acuity. My online dictionary defines acuity as "a sharpness, or keenness of thought, vision or hearing".[22] But the applications of the word are much broader, suggesting acuteness of perception, increased sensitivity or sharpness, an exactitude and discernment of receptivity both in vision and aurally. Leaders need to hear with acuity, as well as being able to clearly share their thoughts and vision with others.

Discernment of what is valid and what is just more "noise" represents an extraordinary challenge for all of us. Acuity becomes more vital in a world investing in hybrid working environments, over-supplied with big data, artificial intelligence and contending with 24-hour news feeds, customer feedback and analytical overload. In a world where social media feeds nudge behaviour, information and misinformation is endemic, and belief in "expert authority" is at a historic low, at the heart of the issue is a matter of trust. How do you establish, build and re-engender trust in teams and organisations? It is a particular challenge for HR and employee communications functions, who have in recent years adopted a more "strategic role", resulting in a move to corporate speak, jargon and sloganeering at the expense of facilitating honest, open, two-way conversations between employers and employees. As companies and individuals adopt AI word generators like ChatGPT, written communications will be viewed with even more scepticism. Decisions on future strategy, marketing choices or a new company purpose need careful consideration, but they also need to be led with verisimilitude and communicated personally with conviction. For leaders trying to take organisations through rapid change, being perceived as someone with real discernment can be hugely powerful.

There are ways leaders can role-model such attentiveness and their acuity can be made more obvious for others. For example, those who seem to see the world with greatest clarity appear to invest much time in exploring it through the eyes and ears of others. It fits with the mode of the glue-minded leader, diversely and widely connected, sensing the pulse, the gossip, the tone and mood of the firm. We need leaders who lead us through the fog. As we enter the next stage of the roaring 20s, we must prepare for thick fog, heavy mist and smoke. Amid much noise, discord and an increasingly politicised debate about trust, leaders in business are most likely to be regarded as a trusted truth-teller, not through their written communication channels, but through the ways they are seen to behave. These leaders will be seen as accessible and actively engaged in different internal and external communities, well read, in touch with society (not just socially well connected) and comfortable with diversity and dissension. They will leave time to explore ambiguity and listen, but, after some reflection, will communicate a clear, compelling, sense of the right ways to tackle the challenges of the future. I concede that this is describing an extraordinarily high bar for the already exhausted leader to aspire to and a leadership style that is rare and unusual.

Authentic leadership

For the past 20 years or so, the management development vogue has been to encourage authentic leadership.

Rob Goffee and Gareth Jones wrote their book *Why Should Anyone Be Led by You*[23] in 2006. The accompanying Harvard Business Review[24] article of the same name is one of the most popular and reprinted HBR papers about leadership ever circulated. It has been hugely influential and its memorable guidance for leaders, using a shorthand reminder of authentic leadership – "be yourself more, with skill" – has inspired thousands of leaders (and leadership course directors) to focus on honing that authenticity.

In being authentic, leaders are not obliged to wear a corporate mask or ill-fitting costume at work, but instead can be vulnerable, open about their doubts, as well as their convictions and feelings. Those leaders with strong regional accents, non-typical heritage, unconventional careers and mistakes made along the way, are encouraged to drop the veneer and be themselves more, but smartly and thoughtfully, with skill. Often, this exhibited authenticity is seen in personal behaviours – particularly an emphasis on being more open with colleagues, and not distinguishing between who you are and how you prefer to behave, at home and at work. The key to this mode of leadership is self-awareness and capitalising on unique signature strengths: being "yourself more, with skill".

Despite this laudable trend emphasising self-awareness, the typical day-to-day function and visible activity of leaders has not changed. You can speak clearly in a meeting with a regional accent, be open about your life outside work and occasionally cry at the water cooler, but the actual activities, function and form of leading and managing have altered very little in the past two decades. People may be more open and willing to express their vulnerability, but that does not make work any less of a grind, or the vagaries of markets, constant change and uncertainty any less of a burden.

The challenge of leading change remains complex, difficult and personally exhausting, but the all-important element of transformational change is galvanising others, not just self. My term "others" (used often in this book) may sound distant and impersonal, but my intention here is a catch-all term for everyone you work with: your boss, peers, colleagues, managers, employees, contacts and anyone else engaged in the wider organisation. These same constituents may also be variously close friends, supporters, allies or detractors, critics, blockers or simply unknown. When you work through the requirements of leading change, even the most straightforward change programme requires an astonishingly broad array of people alignment.

Harness others more with skill

You may begin a change process by clearly articulating why things need to change, but often this requires a perspective from: outside (others); the right people onboard (others); broad engagement to gain momentum (others); visible quick wins (you and others); role modelling the new behaviours needed (you but, in time, not you only); communication broadly, deeply and often across the firm (you, plus very many others);

and structural changes to management, process, systems, resources and capabilities (everyone).

At the heart of this book is an essential immutable reality, that leading organisations is about harnessing others – turning more of your attention to their hopes, dreams, needs and fears. Being smartly attuned to an eco-system of souls is an extraordinary and noble pursuit, and the kind of leadership needed in these disaggregated times. Anything else is just managing, or just administering or just attending. The approach of the glue-minded leader is a higher order of service and experience. It is to "harness others more, with skill".

Being unusual

So, your greater self-awareness and authenticity will only get you so far. In some organisations, being more open and authentic may not even be very distinctive. Authenticity is great, but it does not mean it will create glue. You also need to be able to "harness others more, with skill". As we saw, small and larger groups can be galvanised to achieve remarkable results. My observation, found through working with many interesting leaders is that they had something else in the armory, which made them distinctive. Their trick was that through their day-to-day behaviours, visible actions and ways of working, they were not just authentically expressed, but a little bit unusual compared to the norm around them.

If listening is your super-power, then being unusual is your super-hero costume. It is effortlessly worn, with a few frayed edges and creases, but your difference from the norm is going to be noticed by others and make you stand out, a bit. The power of being unusual should not be underestimated, and this is not about wacky, subversive or extraordinary difference. The simple fact that a leader invests time and effort to create glue will mark them out from others.

Unusual is important, because unusual is rare and therefore gets noticed. Being unusual intrigues peers, colleagues and team members, and make leaders memorable. Be reassured though, the bar for being unusual is not particularly high. You do not need to look, act or behave in a crazy oddball contrarian way. You do not need to cartwheel into the office wearing a scuba-diving suit while whistling La Marseillaise and high-fiving the new recruits. You just have to deviate in small ways from the norm.

Varley rolls up his sleeves

When John Varley became the CEO of Barclays in 2004, after serving a large part of his career there – including a spell as CFO – he had established an image of the archetypal city banker. A lawyer by background, he was known to be from one of the bank's patrician families, a cultured, educated, well-mannered executive, who was well connected and was a trustee of The Prince of Wales's Charitable Foundation. He managed a business of some 60,000 people from a corner office on the 31st floor of the bank's new skyscraper in London's Canary Wharf. Everyone who worked there knew who John Varley was, but few knew John. So, when appointed CEO, he decided to do two very odd things. Unlike the "Global Roadshow CEO", who went large on the communications front, John went small.

Under the Globe Theatre on London's Southbank is a kind of "undercroft" events venue. It's an evocative place, beneath the stage where some of Shakespeare's greatest plays have been performed. John arranged a series of "Chatham House" meetings with small groups of managers and executives of the bank. These were not huge production events, but a simple horseshoe seating array, around a small lit stage. John was interviewed by a business journalist, then spent about an hour answering questions from those he would be leading in his first year as CEO. The sessions were well received, with John coming across as engaging, convivial and refreshingly open, not only about the serious business challenges, but also about the behaviours of some of his trickier direct reports, his struggles to balance work and home life well, and his genuinely held faith and personal beliefs.

Varley had become CEO on the eve of Barclays opening its new head office, One Churchill Place, a stunning workplace. The southside of the building is constructed with an arrangement of six-storey glass atriums, each designed as a flexible meeting space, allowing light to flood the open-plan floors. The workplace is bright, modern and smart. But for many very good reasons, the executive suite, client meeting rooms and hospitality spaces are arranged across the top two floors of the tower, providing great views across to Greenwich Park or along the bend of the river to central London. In 2005, some 5,000 staff moved into the bank's corporate headquarters, but few would normally have access to the executive floor at the top of the tower.

Varley had many qualities as CEO, but also an unusual passion. For table tennis. Every few weeks, as you came into the ground-floor lobby of One Churchill Place, there was a table tennis table set-up. He would send round an email and offer to take on all-comers. His only concession to his usual City-gent look would be the absence of a jacket, and maybe his sleeves rolled-up. He would be fiercely competitive with all and any members of staff who wanted to take him on. It was a quirky, unusual thing to do. What appeared odd behaviour for the CEO was a rare moment of humanity on display for all staff, visitors and other tenants of the building. I only saw him lose a game once, and the small group of staff watching applauded the brave winner!

In two simple ways John Silvester Varley, the archetype City man and FTSE100 CEO, did something unusual: engaging with his senior people as an adult, talking to adults (not just relying on his Comms team for messaging) and, for the thousands of employees who worked at One Churchill Place, their CEO was suddenly seen and heard in a way they would have never expected. These actions had surprising results. His behaviour would be imitated by others, with his direct reports managing their own teams and functions with less formality and more dialogue rather than the previous form of set-piece events. The building atrium spaces were used for departmental socials, informal presentations or for drinks to celebrate clients' wins and other milestones.

His example also seemed to nudge his predecessor as CEO, Matthew W. Barrett. The Chairman of the Barclays group, who had access to a suite of private dining rooms at the top of the building, was regularly spotted queuing with a tray in the staff canteen, joining groups of startled employees for lunch and a chat.

The one exception allowed

While Varley moulded a different image in the eye of his executive team and head-office employees, across the ice-rink of Canada Square, HSBC welcomed a new hire who also proved to be a little unusual. HSBC made what was then a rare move and went outside its normal cohort of stalwart lifetime-serving general managers to hire former P&G executive, Joe Garner, from Dixons Store Group. Garner's appointment to a senior role came with an important brief: to streamline HSBC's portfolio and simplify its range of financial products and services.[25] From the off, everyone could see Joe was bit different from the regular mode of leader and typical management approach at HSBC. Despite not coming through the typical General Manager route of a Hong Kong induction and various far-flung international assignments, Joe still ended up doing well. He was appointed the Head of UK Retail Bank in late 2010 and finally anointed as "one our own" when he was made a Group General Manager, amongst the most senior cadre of leaders at the bank. But it was his difference from the norm that many employees and colleagues noted.

Garner watched and shared TED Talks, which was actually new and unusual in 2006. He would be the hit "top-rated" presenter for new joiner induction (which he regularly led), and was an impressive articulate speaker at internal meetings or when fronting business updates. Garner talked knowledgeably about new tech and trends, customer insight, sustainability and other topical issues, as well as sharing (with a seasoned banker's aplomb) information about risk, governance and financial performance. After the retail banking sector faced much media opprobrium, he championed Treating Customers Fairly in the UK bank and had a popular profile amongst staff even in departments unrelated to his. Staff talked about wanting to work in his part of the bank. None of this on its own seems very remarkable, but his difference in approach amidst the typical form for HSBC management was enough for that difference to be talked about and notable. I asked a senior HR director about Garner, and the way he stood out amongst the other 100 or so managing directors. "Oh, he is the one exception we are allowed," she said.

John Varley and Joe Garner stood out as "different" by doing very little, other than by the small conscious ways in which they chose to show something more of themselves. They were following the Goffee and Jones handbook, being themselves more, with skill.

What is remarkable is how remarkable being slightly "unusual" still appears to be.

Engaging

The need to engage seems obvious, but the glue-creating leader does this broadly, deeply and with a purpose.

As we saw, galvanising is not easy – particularly as change is often perceived as a threat and, being busy and burdened already, you and your best people already have a lot on. So, critical to glue leadership is the ability to maintain energy amongst your best people. Firing them up is one thing, but maintaining connection, collaboration and engagement over time takes commitment, new investment of time and ideas, and a personal amount of "you", which extends beyond geeing them up and watching them go.

You need to be alongside, regularly adding and enhancing the story. Your engagement needs to be purposeful, not just hanging out, walking the floors or lingering in corridors! For that reason, it is important that your investment of time connects with others in ways that feel meaningful, not just manufactured or facile. Later, in Chapter 7, we explore the many ways in which leaders introduce business experiments, or value creation projects, as strategic problems for talented colleagues to wrestle with. My experience is that these are the single best collaborative experiences for your talented people to work on together.

But even without a business experiment, or strategic focus, there are numerous ways in which executives can better engage with more employees and project a better sense of being fully engaged as a leader. A few suggestions (not a comprehensive list by any means) follow.

Learn how to be a mentor

When I first became a Director at Barclays, the Group Chief Information Officer, David Weymouth agreed (perhaps rashly) to be my mentor. David was a very senior person in the group, with a breadth of experience and functional expertise that was light years ahead of mine. Despite the demands of his role, he would meet me for coffee three or four times during the year, listen, ask some helpful questions, gently offer an idea and ensure I knew I could come back to him at any time. As I developed my own corporate stripes and credibility, simply having access to a mentor helped my confidence and, at times, felt invaluable.

If you can, take a professional mentoring course, and develop your listening and coaching skills. You will become known for being generous with your time and it will help you feel better connected too.

Offer to recruit talent for the firm

Many professional services firms have strange organisational quirks — some retaining old-fashioned "lock-step" hierarchies, arcane partnership structures and performance cultures shaped by billable work and long unsociable hours. But they do one thing better than any corporation I have worked with: they take hiring very seriously and it is everyone's job, including the senior partners. These firms need to ensure a pipeline of trainees and associates. They benefit from a marketplace where there are huge numbers of applicants but, at the same time, there is fierce competition amongst the top firms for the very best talent. Leaders in any sector can take something from their approach to recruitment.

If you are a leader interested in glue (and the more senior, the better), then offer to be closely involved in graduate or new entry hiring, not just for your own department or function, but firm wide. Interviewing is a listening discipline and good hiring decisions require discernment. There is fierce competition for new talent and sharpening your advocacy for your firm is a good skill to hone. Over time you will see the benefit of young hires become junior managers, and you will enjoy seeing recruits flourishing and progressing. Moreover, it makes you visibly engaged beyond the norm of your usual responsibilities.

Encourage levity and fun

During the gloomy disruptive days of the Covid-19 pandemic, lots of organisations were unable to meet in person and regular events such as team-offsite, team-lunches and away days were cancelled or, worse, transformed into unimaginative "broadcast" Zoom and Teams meetings. I was struck though by the story of the leadership team at Kellogg's, who arranged for the cost savings made on the physical meeting venue to be spent in other ways. They arranged for all members of the team to get a small sum to hire their own super-hero or movie-star costume. When the CEO hosted the quarterly get together online, he was dressed as a Star Wars character, and he conducted the whole meeting with dozens of colleagues dressed as a sparkling cast of cartoon heroes, comic book villains and interstellar travellers.[26]

If you are charged with organising an internal event for groups of employees, think about how you can put your own personal imprint on it. That might be about taking a few risks or being less "corporate", but remember, being more you with skill, or being "unusual", is one of the best traits of leading with glue.

Show up, unexpectedly

You do not need to bring your table-tennis skills to the company lobby like John Varley, though to be seen unexpectedly where and when it matters most makes a huge difference. I met a number of senior executives who always showed up at a leaving drink or office farewell for departing colleagues. They did not turn up to make a speech or take the limelight, but to genuinely (and briefly) join others in saying thanks and farewell. You cannot underestimate how well that small demonstration of decency will be regarded.

When the CEO of a Swiss bank launched a new major strategy, he did the usual corporate communication cascade, with a presentation to his senior team, and signed-off on a polished internal video, clear internal messaging and a series of smart social media assets. The bank also produced a small "highlights" booklet for all employees, made from recycled materials and embossed with the new mission statement. The CEO liked the book a lot. So, on the day of the strategy launch, he walked every floor, of every department, of every office of the bank in Geneva and distributed the internal post that day, delivering the booklet to every desk and handing it personally to each startled member of staff. No member of staff that day, or the next when he repeated the exercise in Zurich, could have doubted that he did not personally own the new strategy.

If you have an important message to get across, how can you make it feel more personally owned? You do not need to trivialise the message, but what ways can you try to make it feel more human and less corporate?

Small shifts matter

In the examples you have just read, I have simply shared a few stories to illustrate a point: engagement is not about formal communications and messaging; it is about leaders demonstrating personal visibility, their openness and humanity. As a leader, you are on show every day, so the small gestures, changes and signals you send get noticed, are remarked upon and are shared. In my experience, these small shifts – giving time to be a mentor, helping hire talent, encouraging fun, being visible when it matters, and personally owning messaging – all make a huge difference to the sense of you as the leader engaging deeply, differently and with your own personal imprint.

Applying glue

- Why do you think almost all commentaries emphasise the role of the heroic entrepreneur (e.g., Jobs) and not the committed team?
- If you were given a separate building, flying a pirate flag, who would you want to take with you to help create your great idea?
- How could you better use listening as your super-power?
- What is "unusual", but helpful and distinctive, about your leadership style? How could you lean into that more?

Notes and references

1 Definition from https://www.britannica.com/dictionary/galvanize
2 The following were credited with creating the original Macintosh Computer: Peggy Alexio, Colette Askeland, Bill Atkinson, Steve Balog, Bob Belleville, Mike Boich, Bill Bull, Matt Carter, Berry Cash, Debi Coleman, George Crow, Donn Denman, Christopher Espinosa, Bill Fernandez, Martin Haeberli, Andy Hertzfeld, Joanna Hoffman, Rod Holt, Bruce Horn, Hap Horn, Brian Howard, Steve Jobs, Larry Kenyon, Patti King, Daniel Kottke, Angeline Lo, Ivan Mach, Jerrold Manock, Mary Ellen McCammon, Vicki Milledge, Mike Murray, Ron Nicholson Jr., Terry Oyama, Benjamin Pang, Jeff Raskin, Ed Riddle, Brian Robertson, Dave Roots, Patricia Sharp, Burrell Smith, Bryan Stearns, Lynn Takahashi, Guy "Bud" Tribble, Randy Wigginton, Linda Wilkin, Steve Wozniak, Pamela Wyman and Laszlo Zidek.
3 Schlender, B. and Tetzeli, R. (2016) *Becoming Steve Jobs: The Evolution of a Reckless Upstart into a Visionary Leader*. Sceptre, p. 80.
4 Ibid., p. 82.
5 From the "Signing Party", a recollection by Andy Hertzfeld, one of the original Mac team. https://www.folklore.org/StoryView.py?story=Signing_Party.txt
6 Peters, Thomas J. (1982) *In Search of Excellence: Lessons from America's Best-Run Companies*. Harper & Row.
7 *In Search of Excellence* – a documentary produced by John Nathan (1984), based on Tom Peter's bestselling business book that profiled six excellent companies. The segment is about Apple Computers, filmed in the summer of 1984. An excerpt relating to the Macintosh project can be found on YouTube at: https://www.youtube.com/watch?v=l3agg64LM88
8 From *In Search of Excellence*, ibid.

9   Quoted from *In Search of Excellence*, op. cit.

10 Steve Jobs, from *In Search of Excellence*, op. cit.

11 Quoted from *In Search of Excellence*, op. cit.

12 From *In Search of Excellence*, op. cit.

13 Captions from *In Search of Excellence*, op. cit.

14 Retrieved from: https://www.statista.com/statistics/263264/top-companies-in-the-world-by-market-capitalization/

15 In a YouTube extract (2010), where Steve Jobs talks about managing people, 2010. See: https://youtube.com/watch?v=f6odheI4ARg&feature=shares

16 From a TV advertisement, originally narrated by Steve Jobs, for the *Think Different* campaign, created by advertising agency TBWA\Chiat\Day. "Here's to the crazy ones. The misfits. The rebels. The troublemakers. The round pegs in the square holes. The ones who see things differently. They're not fond of rules. And they have no respect for the status quo. You can quote them, disagree with them, glorify, or vilify them. About the only thing you can't do is ignore them. Because they change things. They push the human race forward. And while some may see them as the crazy ones, we see genius. Because the people who are crazy enough to think they can change the world, are the ones who do."

17 Mueller was interviewed in Episode 1 of the TV documentary *The Elon Musk Show*, first shown on BBC TV in November 2022. Episode title: "From South Africa to Silicon Valley – the enigmatic, compelling, and controversial inside story of the world's richest man, as told by family, friends and enemies."

18 Watch the employees' reaction to the first stage of SpaceX's Falcon 9 rocket landing at Cape Canaveral Air Force Station in Florida on 21 December 2015. Retrieved from: https://youtube.com/watch?v=CDXEJMvEl8o&feature=shares

19 Story shared by Jeremy Darroch during a class with the LBS Senior Executive Programme (SEP) cohort in September 2022.

20 Rogers, Carl R. and Roethlisberger, F.J. (November–December 1991) "Barriers, and Gateways to Communication", *Harvard Business Review* magazine. The article originally appeared in *HBR* July–August 1952.

21 You can find Steps at: https://stepsdrama.com

22 Retrieved from: https://languages.oup.com/google-dictionary-en/

23 Goffee, R. and Jones, G. (2006) *Why Should Anyone Be Led by You?* Harvard Business Review Press.

24 See the *HBR* article of the same name: https://hbr.org/2000/09/why-should-anyone-be-led-by-you abstract: "We all know that leaders need vision and energy. But to be inspirational, leaders need four other qualities.

Probably not what you'd expect, these qualities can be honed by almost anyone willing to dig deeply into their true selves."

25 The Times. (27 November 2010) "HSBC Turns Attention to Retail Banking Customers". Retrieved from: https://www.thetimes.co.uk/article/hsbc-turns-attention-to-retail-banking-customers-xnc9nfwjx5q

26 The Kellogg's story is courtesy of Peter Hinssen, Founder of nexxworks, a guest lecturer at London Business School (see www.nexxworks.com).

6

CREATING GLUE

Leaders can use key meetings during the year to create glue amongst the senior team. But what works well and what deflates?

We have covered a lot of ground already: discovering, describing and defining glue; then exploring the important leadership behaviours that create glue; and highlighting those which may mark out your leadership style as (a little) unusual. Our focus on glue this far has been particularly concerned with engaging and connecting talented people from across the organisation. But what can you do to create glue at the top of the organisation, amongst your own senior team?[1]

I am sure that you would consider your senior leadership team as an array of many talents, ready to be galvanized, excited about the future and more focused on delighting your customers? I sincerely hope that is the case. The Japanese have a nice phrase that roughly translates as the "fish rots from the head".[2] In other words, the tone and example set from the top of the organisation permeates down through the firm, good and bad. If glue

DOI: 10.4324/9781003410690-7

can be a feature of the way the top team works, this can only be a good thing when you seek to cultivate it elsewhere.

One way senior leaders can cultivate some glue-creation amongst themselves is to make resolving organisational problems a focus for their own leadership development. For example, you might consider using signature internal events during the year such as team off-sites, leadership workshops and strategy planning days, as a way of demonstrating the importance of glue. Ideally, you can make the idea of glue better understood and be more clearly felt amongst the senior team.

The tone set at the top is important, as it sends powerful signals to the rest of the firm. One of the most important ways in which the tone is set, and is then made to permeate, is in the senior team's response to change, particularly the execution of a new strategy. I will offer a broad observation about strategy execution and the importance of the top team's role.

Too often a new strategy is thoughtfully devised after many months, grounded in careful analysis of the market and future opportunities. The leadership team are briefed, and then the strategy is communicated across the organisation. But then it flounders, and is ultimately sunk, though a lack of real leadership commitment to its execution. When senior teams come together to meet, particularly to talk about strategy and change, it is important that agreement about the direction and the impact of change is both explicitly agreed and committed to beyond the end of the leaders' discussion, and is enacted and supported in its implementation. It is critical that the CEO and senior team have confidence that they will execute strategy through a team with the same priorities and a shared sense of mission and purpose. This is not always the case, but it is vitally important.

This is a key challenge for any organisation and its leaders. In some ways, it is the challenge.

A tale of two workshops

Often this challenge comes sharply into focus during a leadership team's annual offsite, or strategy workshop. These meetings can be great moments for the firm, providing powerful clarity and conviction amongst the senior team. Too often though they fail to achieve very much, and many participants dread the predictable format and experience of taking part. Over the years I have formulated a set of principles about how such meetings should be organised, led and delivered. But before diving into that, I think two pivotal experiences are worth sharing: one which highlights how much damage a badly convened team workshop can do; and the other showing how the hidden capabilities within under-pressure teams can be harnessed to great effect.

In short, one day ended in tears. The other ended up being the making of careers.

Workshop 1: The mad scientist

The first meeting was held about a decade ago in a London hotel, with the Managing Director of the business bringing together his direct reports who were the various "heads of function" from across the whole group. The organisation was re-engineering at pace to a new model of operation, which would provide "clarity, efficiency and economy". Or rather, that's what it said on the printed joining instructions. Unfortunately, I am not sure anyone truly bought the new model before getting out of the cab that morning. No one seemed to have been pre-briefed or properly prepared for what was to come. For several of the participants, it seemed the Managing Director was determined to put the group through some sort of "mad scientist" psychological experiment by convening a workshop where contrary views were simply ignored and alternative ideas dismissed.

Without a facilitator to guide the discussion, conflict was quickly brought to the surface, and two close colleagues aggressively faced off in a way I had not seen before. One left the room in tears. As far as I know, the rift created that day – amidst a mess of flipcharts, divergent arrows and whiteboard marker pens – remains. After two days of debating and re-plotting the implementation of a change process that no one clearly believed in, the leadership team stumbled out into the air, exhausted, frustrated and as incoherent a team as when they had arrived. Fifteen people. Forty-eight hours of head-banging. Nothing achieved. Colleagues' relationships were damaged, and a rudderless team left floundering. The Managing Director pressed on with his agenda, regardless, but the business and its shareholders surely deserved better?

Workshop 2: Saving the sinking ship

Ten years later, a different business and a different team offsite. With its reputation at risk, the business had been rocked by a series of seismic shocks more dangerous than the "usual" vagaries of markets, clients and regulators. The business was reeling with complex management challenges. The very essence of the organisation's brand was founded on exceptional standards of propriety, trust and integrity. And now it seemed to have been holed below the water line, and panic was setting in.

The two-day workshop was a revelation, and I witnessed a leadership team strengthened by the experience. The business was run by a CEO who took huge amounts of time and energy to engage the team and listened to differing views ahead of the workshop. He did not use the event to mandate the steps that would need to be implemented or simply to introduce the consultants who would engineer a route out of the malaise. He set out the problems before the managers, looking to the team for more ideas, for solutions and practical steps that would need to be owned and acted upon in the weeks ahead.

The meeting was facilitated independently and rigorously, so that views could be aired and discussed, but ultimately so that decisions could be made. Those decisions were captured clearly during the workshop and syndicated immediately. Many of the team grew in experience, stature and status in the months ahead. There was much trepidation and uncertainty heading into that workshop, but the coherence created was tangible. The business did take some time to grow and thrive again after that session, but it achieved the main objectives in the CEO's mind: survive and build again.

Bringing teams together to shape a strategy and navigate future business opportunities or organisational problems, can be pivotal moments for senior teams. It can also be time-consuming, risky and unproductive if these forums are not carefully thought through and led with expertise. Think about your next offsite or workshop. How does your leader engage with her or his team? When you work together on a strategy workshop, does the meeting design and facilitation leave space for contributions and alternative perspectives, or just press on with a pre-determined process? Are newer team members brought into the fold, without the trial of having to politically earn their spurs? Are younger "next generation" perspectives brought into the mix? The very positive workshop experience mentioned here, in stark contrast to the "mad scientist" workshop a decade earlier, showed me that a leader can imprint their own personality and values simply by making the workshop a little more like themselves at their best: open, professional and involving.

So how might we use events like this to generate oodles of glue amongst the leadership team of the firm?

Senior teams are like families

For the senior team, a slightly different approach is needed than when engaging talent from across the business. This not to say your peers and colleagues are not also very talented; it is just, as peers and colleagues, they are likely to respond somewhat differently to your sudden evangelism for creating glue. If you were to (inadvisedly) decide to go ahead and click through your well-prepared PowerPoint on "How to Create Glue", my expectation is that you will find very few in your audience "suspending disbelief".

Unfortunately, glue is harder to create here amongst the established leadership group than it is in harnessing talented strangers. You and your colleagues are deeply immersed in the real challenges of the business, and that need to constantly deliver, wrestling with the "here and now", makes it difficult to step back and reflect objectively on the challenges ahead. You also already know one another way too well, at least in a transactional sense.

Senior teams are often mired in the day-to-day grind of delivery, and the personal relationships (good and bad) in the team are shaped by the collective bumps and bruises that the struggle of "getting things done" creates. A CEO once merrily told me of his senior team, "We're like a band of brothers and sisters", only for me to enter the room and meet a set of distant cousins amongst a blended family of adopted offspring, and soon-to-be-divorced reluctant couples, huddled around a flipchart, praying for the weekend to end. Of course, I exaggerate the point, but even amongst the most mature and close-knit teams, there will have been some sharp elbows, cross words, much history and politics aplenty.

The shit of yesterday

Peter Hinssen, guest faculty at LBS and founder of nexxworks, is a serial entrepreneur, writer, speaker and advisor on disruptive technology, future trends and business transformation. He meets with, and presents to, more business leaders around the world than just about anyone I have ever known.

In his book *The Day After Tomorrow*,[3] Peter describes the endemic tendency of senior leadership teams to be too focused on today, and the legacy issues of yesterday, rather than those of tomorrow. Senior teams are often mired in the operational issues of the enterprise, and the relationships in the team are often shaped by past internal battles, not future focused opportunities. He advocates a stretch to our thinking, where leaders spend more of their time together and collective energies on the "day after tomorrow", not the current, or legacy issues of the business – which he was bluntly advised by a client to re-label as the "shit of yesterday".

A deliberate shift and concerted effort are needed to get the team together to focus on the future and wrestle open-mindedly with the themes, trends and (what Hinssen now calls) the "vibes" that are shaping the landscape for firms in the future. How do leaders operate in and succeed amidst the change leadership challenges that the future creates? Sometimes it is healthy to park the day-to-day reporting, quarterly updates, budget cycle and risk review, find some fresh air, create some headspace and, as a senior team, get busy creating some glue by thinking and talking about tomorrow and (hopefully) the day after tomorrow.

For me, opportunities to gather a group of leaders together with an agenda like that is leadership development nirvana, and a rare chance to create glue.

The annual offsite

Much time, effort and angst are put into the annual senior leadership meeting, whether called an offsite, strategy workshop, leadership conference or even a retreat. Unfortunately, few of these events manage to deliver much value or create glue. I know from designing and facilitating numerous forums like this, that many leaders look forward to the annual "offsite" with all the excitement of a trip to the dentist.

The meeting may be given a different name each year but, for the senior team, the experience too often feels like the same old ground covered, with the same topics in the same gloomy room as before. If managed well, these workshops can be pivotal for the business, providing clarity on strategy, conviction amongst the senior team and a real platform for the

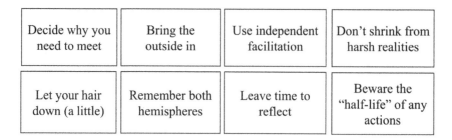

Decide why you need to meet	Bring the outside in	Use independent facilitation	Don't shrink from harsh realities
Let your hair down (a little)	Remember both hemispheres	Leave time to reflect	Beware the "half-life" of any actions

Figure 6.1 The critical elements for successful leadership offsites

CEO to create momentum. Too often though the workshop fails, and many participants resent the predictable format and experience of taking part. While a laudable objective of bringing the senior team together might be to build greater collaboration and break-down silos, the actual experience too often serves to highlight a heightened sense of being apart.

Over the years, I have learned more about how leadership workshops should be best organised, led and delivered. I have also wrestled in detail with the particular issues of team dynamics, psychology, environment, setting, format, room layout, content design and so on, to create a workshop that actually energises participants. There are numerous organisational and practical "hygiene" factors that are important before, during and after the meeting. But it is the big principles of design that matter in ensuring coherence of the event and any good chance of a productive outcome. I have called these elsewhere the "Magnificent Seven" rules for leadership meetings (although as you read on you will realise there is a bonus eighth rule tucked in at the end). But this is less to do with their magnificence and more to do with that badge being more memorable than seven dwarves, or seven virtues.

Key principles for leadership team meetings

For brevity here, I have highlighted the seven factors that are critical – the first of which you should consider before you even consider setting a date.

1. Decide why the team needs to meet

Before you get into determining what needs to be on the agenda, who should attend and where you will hold the workshop, consider carefully: why should you bother meeting at all? An hour spent discussing (in a structured way) with the CEO why she wants to get the senior team together may well be a more valuable conversation than the subsequent 48 hours spent in a country-house hotel embroiled in a circular debate which frustrates both participants and the same CEO.

Unfortunately, the key question of "Why meet?" is, in my experience, seldom clearly resolved before the organising team is already deep into the detail of inviting speakers, chasing presentations and confirming dietary requirements. The answer to "Why meet?" can often refocus the agenda on a very small number of critical reasons for meeting, rather than a long list of competing business objectives, targets and internal issues. A real clarity of focus, summarised, agreed and maintained throughout the subsequent planning of the workshop can be invaluable. No one enjoys their time being wasted, so be brutal in editing the agenda back to the core issues at stake. If there is any space left, leave it blank; there are other ways the team can use that time.

2. Bring the outside in

Often the agendas for leadership workshops are too inward looking, re-reporting on the numbers, project updates, the perennial cost-challenges and complex resourcing issues. While these may be worthy topics to discuss in other forums, I have found that there is more participant engagement generated by looking outside the organisation – seeking to be better understand the customers, competitors, future trends and market dynamics that will shape what the business will face in the future.

I once worked with Prudential, a major insurance group in the UK. During their leadership conference, and without any warning, a large group of real customers arrived and joined the tables with the executives. This was not an infiltration of protesters, as each had been invited to join part of the leadership programme to meet the senior leaders and talk openly about their experience of the firm, its services and their hopes for the future.

It was group of young and old, diverse, from across the UK, representing a sample of the firms' real-life customer base, literally sat at the same table. Suddenly, the design and marketing of insurance products ceased to be an abstract discussion and became something grounded in questions about service and value, transparency and trust. It was a brave move by the marketing executive who co-ordinated that part of the workshop, but the insights gained were compelling and the learning experience for all involved was long lasting.

Other ways of bringing the outside in are perhaps less literal, but there is real value in sourcing unusual external speakers that the audience are unfamiliar with, or from firms and sectors, markets and diverse perspectives that might challenge and surprise. Guest contributors, if used at all, should serve to open minds, not induce yawns. So, when devising the agenda, the glue creating question to be asked, is "How does this help us to look at the business from the outside-in?" Some of the best ideas for this can sourced from customer service staff who deal with real-time issues and feedback, and from "next generation" employees who have a different perspective on what works, what resonates and what is being seen and shared by customers, particularly online and on social media.

3. Use independent facilitation

If the workshop brings together disparate colleagues from around the business, and sometimes from around the planet, how do you ensure that all perspectives are properly heard? If the plan is simply to "broadcast news" and have a convivial dinner, then job done. But this narrow format often creates deep frustration. Sometimes a team needs another way of thinking through the issues and a conduit to bring the group together. Often the route to collaborative decision making is through employing professional facilitation which can improve the continuity and productivity of the workshop.

There are a number of other advantages to this – not least that the CEO and business heads are able to participate fully in discussions, and not feel obliged to steer and manage the workshop itself, as well as the "housekeeping" that might entail. A skilled facilitator can ask the questions in the room that no one else may feel comfortable to raise and ensure wide participation in the group, providing some ground to air monitoring of the more vocal contributors. At their best a good facilitator can bring into the debate a sense of the outside – the "reality check" that sometimes cuts through the nonsense.

4. Don't shrink from bold harsh realities

The workshop should be an opportunity for leaders to talk through issues openly and candidly, not politically or circumspectly. Such openness does not come naturally amongst a charged senior and political cohort, but exceptionally, when it does, the results have been impressive. The learning here is born out of hard-won experience. I have been involved in organising off-sites and workshops which have unfortunately coincided with a catastrophic market crash, the shock resignation of a key leader, a hostile corporate action, a major media scandal and news of recent fatalities in the workplace.

These were difficult experiences bringing into very sharp focus the merit, if any, of having the leadership team holed-up together when the "real-world" issues in the markets or local communities were being so acutely felt. But we also found that these were pivotal moments of demonstrable leadership for the key figures in those firms addressing the issues with clear and personal ownership. Rob Goffee and Gareth Jones, in their book *Why Should Anyone Work Here?*,[4] advocate that leaders practice "radical honestly" in the stewardship of their firms.[5]

For them, the importance of "high levels of trust" within complex matrix organisations is paramount and key to this is "open and honest information sharing". It should not take the circumstance of a sudden crisis to generate radical honesty amongst leadership teams, but where I have seen it happen in real time, the effect has been powerful in steering a more unified response. The glue-creating leader also benefits from the information flows within their networks. Goffee and Jones encourage leaders to have more "radically honest" conversations about people's hopes and fears throughout the organisation.

Power relationships tends to sanitise the information that reaches the top. You need to find a way of knowing what's really going on. Take a deep dive in to your organisation. Collecting information that has not been sanitised. Call people to bring you bad news – make it safe for them. Radical honesty works both ways.[6]

5. Let your hair down (a little)

My experience is that the uniform of the typical business offsite is that the men look like the clothes section of John Lewis in the UK – all smart chinos and polo tops, branded jumpers and new deck shoes. Which is fine; I am no sartorial expert, though you will recall the playful executives at Kellogg's, online, dressed as superheroes and movie actors (Chapter 5). Without even going that far, what can you do that would allow your participants to express a little more of themselves? When leading with glue, it is OK to be a little unusual.

I attended one offsite with an Indian Diaspora business, where the various executives took it in turn to sing after dinner. Genuinely, they each sang, while others listened. At another, the organiser announced different segments of the agenda like the Geordie-accented narrator of the TV show *Big Brother*. At another, in the swanky setting of The Mandarin Hotel in Geneva, the organisers hired a group of British actors called "Spanner in The Works" to infiltrate the waiting staff and serve dinner badly, spilling drinks, tripping and causing mayhem as the evening went on. The act brought home, in a hilarious way, the reality of customer service, which had been a theme of the conference throughout. At another, the organiser hired a professional magician to walk through the evening reception doing card tricks with a group of investment managers. The jaw-dropping punch line was not his dexterity with cards, but the number of wallets, ties and jewellery he had pick-pocketed and then elegantly handed back the CEO and others at the end of the evening. Again, I think there was a memorable business metaphor somewhere in the exercise, but I was more relieved to have my cufflinks returned.

Bringing music, performance or comedy to a business event does not have to be like that episode of the UK version of *The Office*, where David Brent brought his guitar to the workshop, played and made everyone die inside. You might take a few gentle risks, ensuring that you offend no one, and encourage the team to bring back some levity and colour and light to proceedings. Working life, even amongst a business leadership team, can seem "nasty, brutish and short", so why not find a way to laugh about the perversity of it all together.

6. Remember both hemispheres

Not every offsite needs an exploration of MBTI personality types,[7] or some other psychological tool, but as a base minimum you should remember that all members of your audience come equipped with both a left and right side to their brain. If you bombard the group with data, some will be invigorated and some instantly bored. Ask the team to "paint the future on canvas" and those with a more rational vent may be equally bemused (though may not say as much outloud). In my experience, most workshops spend the majority of the time spent on numbers, forecasts, charts, analytical input and an over-emphasis on looking backwards, for a guide to future performance.

Workshops are more effective for all participants when this rational approach is appropriately balanced with creative exercises for brainstorming, decision-making and prioritisation, as well entertaining ways of exploring teamwork and collaboration. These should be managed professionally; no one should be physically stressed or brought to tears, even though I have seen that happen. When facilitated effectively, even the most data-conscious introspective types will still respond positively to the challenge of thinking about the future in a different way.

7. Leave time to reflect

Building in any time for reflection amidst a myriad of competing demands on a busy workshop schedule is a major challenge. In my experience it almost never happens. Unless it is carved out in some well-meaning "well-being" session at 7am, reflection does not get programmed on leadership workshops. I worked with a large senior team of a large natural resources company in the spring of 2015. The hotel and conference venue for the meeting formed part of a 200-acre estate, with spectacular vistas, lakes and roaming deer. The place was beautiful, with a rich history (the Magna Carta was first distributed nearby at Runnymede some 800 years earlier). Despite the evocative setting, the programme agenda was timetabled so intensely that the opportunity to explore, to stroll or to "shoot the breeze" with one another was restricted to drinks on the terrace on the last night of the meeting. The executives had flown in from all over the world. Surely, an opportunity missed.

Research has shown that reflection is key to embedding learning and understanding. This is not about just going for an idle walk around the block between presentations; it can be facilitated in small groups and properly structured. Even time scheduled for a walk would be valuable in itself and send an important signal to leaders on how their reflection time with one another was regarded as value-creating.

8. Beware the danger of the "half-life" action planning

The bonus eighth rule is about what happens next. You will recognise the scene. The flipcharts are full to bursting with scribbles, arrows, sticky notes and creative invention. The CEO has thanked the participants and wished them a safe journey home. The workshop is over for another year. Immediately, anything of value that has been agreed during the workshop is in mortal danger of decaying within days. I believe that it is vitally important to immediately capture decisions and outputs from discussions and provide these succinctly within hours (not days) of the completion of the workshop. It should be produced in a format that can be easily shared – not simply forwarded by email without a sense of co-authorship or ownership – and shared through personal face-to-face briefings by leaders with their teams.

A rare opportunity to create glue

Bringing leadership teams together to navigate future business issues can be productive and energising. It can also be time-consuming, risky and unproductive if not carefully thought through and led with expertise. Before thinking through your next offsite or workshop, what has been the default format for these events in the past, and how have they been perceived? Check out the evaluation and if you cannot find any, interview some who attended last time and probe gently. What was the most valuable aspect of most people attending? Did the previous workshop design and facilitation style leave space for contributions and alternative perspectives? Or did it just press on with a pre-determined agenda? Were newer team members brought warmly into the fold, without the trial of having to politically earn their spurs? An informal discussion with recent past participants, particularly those relatively new to the organisation, may shed much light.

Whatever that past experience, there are many ways in which you can design your next workshop with a more engaging format and style. The best leadership workshops I have been involved with have addressed a limited number of objectives, but at their heart enabled the CEO to impart something of their own values into their team, simply by making the workshop a little more like themselves at their best: energising, positive and engaging. When the tone is set from the top, then the wider adoption of good practice into regular team meetings, department updates and town halls can be a beneficial outcome for all employees.

The hidden benefit to these events is a better dynamic amongst the team – a chance to connect across different parts of the organisation, and line of sight towards customer and client concurs, rather than organisational issues. Be intentional about that. Make the sessions about glue. Even get the CEO or most senior person amongst the group to talk about the ingredients of glue: better collaboration, identification of talent, taking time to listen and creating cohorts from across the business.

The annual leadership offsite might not necessarily create commercial value, but hopefully some organisational and personal value can be drawn from the time invested. The real glue-creating opportunity, though, is elsewhere: in harnessing the collaborative skills of your most talented employees in what are known as business experiments.

That is where the real gold lies, as well as the glue.

Applying glue

- How do you spend time with your senior colleagues? On operational issues and business performance, or on the themes, trends and ideas that will shape the future of the business?
- How can you ensure that time spent together is not just forward looking, but also scrutinises the organisation from the outside-in?
- What does "letting your hair down (a little)" look like for you and your team?

Notes and references

1 Elements of Chapter 6 incorporate some recommendations first shared in an article for LBS. Dore, John. (19 June 2017) "The secret of brilliant leadership workshops", LBS Think online. https://www.london.edu/think/the-secret-of-brilliant-leadership-workshops

2 Garratt, Bob. (2010) *The Fish Rots from The Head: The Crisis in our Boardrooms: Developing the Crucial Skills of the Competent Director.* Profile Books.

3 Hinssen, Peter. (2017) *The Day After Tomorrow: How to Survive in Times of Radical Innovation.* nexxworks. See also materials and resources at www.peterhinssen.com and at www.nexxworks.com

4 Goffee, R. and Jones, G. (2015) *Why Should Anyone Work Here?: What It Takes To Create An Authentic Organization.* Harvard Business Review Press.

5 Ibid., pp. 51–74.

6 Ibid., p. 74.

7 The purpose of the Myers-Briggs Type Indicator (MBTI) personality inventory is to make the theory of psychological types described by C.G. Jung understandable and useful in people's lives. The tool is very often used in leadership teams to gauge difference in preferences exhibited amongst teams. www.myersbriggs.org

7

EXPERIMENTING WITH GLUE

Using experiments is a powerful way to create glue amongst disparate teams, generating innovation to better serve customers and improve business outcomes.

Using business experiments is one of the most effective ways to create glue, as the format and process of experimentation is a smart way to harness talent – sparking new ideas, supporting innovation, and offering new ways of working to better serve customers and improve business outcomes. Using experiments as a way of configuring talent can in itself be a form of organisational development – breaking down barriers, creating bonds across boundaries and encouraging talented staff, who would normally be unconnected, to work together with their peers on thorny business problems.

Why experiments create glue

Experiments have become an integral part of many of the customised learning programmes for executives attending London Business School.

DOI: 10.4324/9781003410690-8

Some of this experimentation was initially born out of the work of Professors Gary Hamel and Julian Birkinshaw at LBS, through what they called The Management Innovation Lab[1] and their work with corporate clients, in particular with Roche,[2] to experiment and innovate with them around their management practices. Others have taken experiments and built them as essential components of learning programme design, making the process of experimentation itself part of the learning experience.

The best way to learn about experimentation is, of course, by experimenting, but there is also some very helpful theory and practice that has been developed which can guide your approach. My fellow Executive Education contributors and colleagues Rob James, Jules Goddard, Andrew MacLennan, Linda Irwin and Giles Ford have each developed and run numerous powerful learning experiences, which incorporate "value-creation" experiments, coaching participating executives through a systematised process of experimentation, which often creates measurable results.

For more insights into the background, thinking and execution of experiments, there is an excellent explanation of the theory and practice in *Business Experimentation: A Practical Guide for Driving Innovation and Performance in Your Business*, by Rob James and Jules Goddard.[3] Rather than the traditional Business School approach of exploring cases, models and management theories, their radical learning methods encouraged participants to act, applying learning practically and making an impact. Their approach has helped thousands of managers look critically at their thorny business issues and awkward strategic questions. These are framed as "business challenges", and are followed with a systematic process used to test ideas and explore possible solutions.

As well as inculcating learning in themselves, such experiments can also be highly productive in creating glue, through colleagues collaborating in different ways (to their typical interactions the workplace). This is because of the way particular experiments are devised and executed, and the underpinning thinking for this is worth a quick overview.

As the pace of change increases, we often talk of the need to foster agility and generate more innovative thinking in our organisations. Dr Andrew MacLennan puts the case for using experiments neatly:

> Whilst other forms of research, analysis, planning, and execution remain very useful, for some organisational challenges, these approaches cannot

provide quick enough answers. Rather than calculate, predict, assume, and estimate, it can be better to explore, try, test, learn and refine.[4]

To create glue, you need to have more of your talented people doing the latter – exploring, trying, testing, learning and refining. Experience has shown that if you get your talented employees to collaborate on important meaningful experiments and, if they are set up in the right way, the results can be tangible and the glue will then follow. It fits something of the "configuration" requirements that Sumantra Ghoshal wrote about (see Introduction) – connecting those with social capital, giving them access to one another's perspective, providing a sense of anticipation and a focus around which they might cohere. The experiments are framed as important and value-creating, not frivolous, and with strategic importance and clear senior executive sponsorship, there is some motivation for participants to follow-through and deepen their collaboration. Experiments are also designed in a way that helps team members not normally connected with one another to work better in combination.

Experiments are usually conducted on a small scale at first, making them easier and faster to implement than typical business changes. They are also designed to give quick results, so they are sometimes termed "fail-fast" experiments. Experiments can be used to test conscious or proactive changes to how a particular business practice is done or, more simply, test customer preferences – for example, using online A/B testing. While the experiment itself might be small, the scope of people brought together in the process can be broad and (normally) disparate, ensuing a diversity of perspectives is brought together. Experiments are also by their nature bespoke, being directly tuned to relate to the thorny business problems within the firm and, therefore, they attract executive ownership and interest. Since the intent of these experiments is about improving business outcomes (saving costs, streamlining processes or improving the customer experience), they are sometimes called "value-creation" experiments. A third route is to undertake individual leadership experiments – for example, making a conscious change to your personal style of working and gauging the results.

While these individual experiments have some value, where would be the glue in that? Experiments are best curated as collaborative experiences, connecting colleagues from around the world to explore the far horizon and consider the external context for the organisation now and, crucially, in the future. The strategy and growth agenda of many businesses depends upon developing organisation-wide leadership capacity to accelerate key initiatives, seize opportunities for growth and to increase innovation across the business. Experiments allow for this without huge expense, international assignments or lengthy secondments, and the insights found can be shared widely as part of the process. If some participants find the idea of experimentation a wholly novel approach, then this can take some adjustment in thinking, particularly the value placed on failing fast. Likewise, for participants who want to feel stretched, they can be designed to be accelerated challenges, requiring a very quick understanding of the approach, a speedy process of execution and agile behaviours to involve and engaged others.

A few key principles

When we think of experiments, our first thought might be of the science lab, but the focus here is some aspect of a real business that needs to be tested – for example, to gauge customer interest or new product ideas. Andrew MacLennan describes the value of experiments in this way:

> Experiments usually test a predetermined "hypothesis", though you do not have to have any certainty that the hypothesis is correct. In fact, experiments leading to a hypothesis being rejected are still regarded as successful because they create insight. It is fine for an idea to be "proved wrong" as this knowledge is used to inform further experiments or wider organisational decisions.[5]

As Jules Goddard has demonstrated,[6] experiments are not the same as "projects", where there are clear and anticipated outcomes and specified deliverables at the outset. As they are not an extension of existing planned work, they also allow the topic, focus or area of interest to be wide, and not restricted to areas which may already have investment and defined objectives. They allow leaders to "curiously wander and wonder" exploring ideas that might seem quirky or tangential. As such, they suit sponsorship by the glue-minded leader who is trying to galvanise the best energies and interests of people, not just burden them with more tasks. They also serve an inherent gap not normally found in day-to-day process and activities by unleashing talent to better serve the organisation and by bringing the very best of themselves and their talents to the task.

Experiments also work best when they are bold, or even when they test an idea that might seem a little controversial. A famous hypothesis once tested by an experiment in a large pharmaceutical company was framed as follows: "If all expense claims were visible to all employees, then there would no longer be a need for approval systems."[7] You can imagine how that might get some attention amongst the management team.

The innovative experiments run by Rob James, Jules Goddard and others at LBS have created real substantive value for their sponsoring organisations. I worked with one organisation which, as an experiment, simply wanted to test some hypothesis about how the choice of colour of a product might change the propensity to buy. They added the existing product with new product options to the firm's website using a mock-up page. If the customer tried to select the new (as yet unavailable colour choice), they received a "404 error" message, which although not a great customer experience immediately provided a data point for the experiment team. The team were able to capture the data very quickly on the customer's likely propensity to buy a product that did not yet exist. They were able therefore to make some informed decisions before they sent instructions on product colour selection to the production line. The experiment cost very little but provided a useful insight before manufacture had started.

The "404 test" is a small example, but experiments can also be astronomically valuable and global-market transformingly enormous. Gary Hamel tells a great story about the extraordinary impact of one such experiment at Amazon, an organisation that prides itself on its culture of innovation and experimentation. As he recounts, it was apparently not always that way.

> More than a decade ago, at Amazon, a young employee called Greg Linden had this idea that Amazon could mine some of their data and they could give buyers recommendations. Amazon would look at what you and others were buying, and then say you might also be interested in some other things. Greg took this idea to his boss who told him, "No way, we're not going to do that. Our whole ethos is simplicity – you've heard of 'one click' right? We're not going to put anything in front of our buyers; we just let them check out." Well, Greg went and did the experiment anyway, went against his boss and the results were kind of incredible . . . now every e-commerce company in the world has something like that. But talking about it later, here's what Greg said: "In my experience,

innovation can only come from the bottom. Those closest to the problem are in the best position to solve it. Everyone, everyone must be able to experiment, learn and iterate. Position, obedience, tradition, they should hold no power." Could you imagine your CEO saying that?[8]

Experiments as collaborative opportunities

Business experiments can be designed and carried out individually, but where would be the fun (or for that matter the glue) in that? Teamwork is crucial, connecting different perspectives, skills, learning styles, experience and stakeholder connections. These elements all play their part in explaining why diverse teams run great experiments. You can test a hypothesis – for example, the potential customer appetite for a new product online in one market – and simultaneously have a colleague run the same experiment in a different market to compare results. The "fast-fail" nature of the experiment can excite the curious and satisfy the easily bored, as results come back quickly. Normally disparate individuals, brought together into experiment teams, collaborate around a process which can be deeply engaging, as they explore, try, test, learn and refine.

The definitive value of experimentation, as part of an executive development programme, was brought home to me in a profound way in 2017, when I was asked to work with Husqvarna Group, an innovative products and services business, headquartered in Scandinavia. But before we head to Stockholm to find out more about their brief for a new learning programme, I need to share a little of the back story to explain why investment in future leadership capability was important to the Group and its CEO.

Kai Wärn takes the reins at Husqvarna Group

In 2013, when Kai Wärn was brought into Husqvarna Group as CEO, he inherited a business at a low ebb. He quickly commissioned a CEO survey of the top 100 managers in the Group to better understand the internal climate and found the results sobering. The famed margins which had historically made Husqvarna the "star" of the Electrolux Group (from which it was spun off in 2006) were a thing of the past, and the strategy was faltering. Over the next few months, several key roles, including Chief Financial Officer, Chief Technology Officer and Business Development VP, were appointed and two new senior executives were hired into the Group. Wärn set about a rigorous turnaround programme, called the Accelerated Improvement Programme, which emphasised cost rationalisation and profit pool focus, and launched a new strategy and organisation aimed at market leadership and doubling the operating margin in three years.

As well as market and product leadership, Wärn wanted to build on the Group's strength as one of "thought leadership" in their chosen markets, harnessing a 325-year history of product innovation and new ideas. Husqvarna Group remains, three centuries after its creation, a business founded on continuous innovation, with a succession of products evolving over time: from making rifles for the Swedish army, to sewing machines, kitchen appliances, classic motorcycles, lawnmowers, chainsaws, concrete cutters, battery-powered tools and lawnmowers.[9] Innovation had traditionally come through the Group's expertise in mechanical engineering, but as the launch of its top-selling robotic devices demonstrated, new ideas would increasingly have to come through software, a broader service offering, and a re-imagining of customer needs and insights. Although various strategic initiatives were being led centrally, Wärn was certain that not all the best ideas would come "top-down" from the general management team into the business, and he was convinced of the need to invest in future leadership capabilities now to create leaders who "empower others to look forwards, who consider future needs strategically, and see their point of departure, the ideas and forces that can shape the future".[10]

Wärn said that it was important that talented people were explicitly understood to have a career with the wider Group, not just their current division, so the time was right now to invest in the development of a future group of leaders, from all parts of the business. He would expect to be personally involved in the development programme, but passed the design and launch of what was to become the "Future Executive Programme" to two of his senior team, who were both, at that time, leading the Human Resources function: Leigh Dagberg and Per Ericson.

A programme for senior leaders

The Husqvarna Group headquarters are accessed via an anonymous door in an unremarkable street in central Stockholm (Sweden). You would have no real sense of the firm, its products or its history from the street outside, but as you enter its brightly lit lobby, you immediately notice the enormous pink chainsaw on the reception desk. Behind on the wall is a timeline of product innovation since 1689, from rifles, motorcycles, the world's first solar-powered lawnmower and vibration free chainsaw, diamond tools and demolition robots.

The Husqvarna Group are known as leading global producers of outdoor power products and innovative solutions for forest, park and garden care. Today their products include chainsaws, trimmers, robotic lawn mowers (of which it is a global market leader) and ride-on lawn mowers. Husqvarna Group are also leaders in equipment and diamond tools for the construction and stone industries. The Group's products and solutions are sold under brands including Husqvarna, Gardena and Orbit via direct sales, dealers and retailers to consumers and customers in more than 100 countries. Around 14,000 employees in 40 countries currently make up this smart, progressive and innovative modern company.

When I met the leadership team in the summer of 2016, Husqvarna Group were successful, profitable and had a clear agreed plan for the next couple of years. However, like many companies with a heritage of innovation, the question was: "What next?" Per and Leigh invited London Business School to design and deliver a new custom executive programme for selected direct reports to the Husqvarna Group's Management Committee, as well as outstanding high-potential leaders identified for future succession. Sixteen senior managers from around the world were selected to join the development programme, hosted at LBS in London. Per and Leigh wanted their future leaders engaged in a search for innovation, customer insight, digital services, new technologies and innovation – elements that would shape their markets and business in the future. Included in the programme design brief were future thinking, executing strategy and collaboration to realise the strengths of the Group. Tim Sylvester at LBS designed the programme, and I became involved in facilitating and delivery, working closely with Per and Leigh who came to London with their talented cohort in late 2017.

Paving the way

Early in the week the programme participants from Husqvarna spent some time with Laurence Kemball-Cook, the founder of Pavegen,[11] a technology company that creates clean electricity through the kinetic energy from pedestrian footfall. Kemball-Cook's story of invention and innovation felt fresh and imaginative. It was also one of repeated experimentation.

After initially winning permission to install a prototype of his kinetic tiles at The Westfield Shopping centre, near to the London Olympic Park in 2012, Kemball-Cook took the learning from that and re-iterated. He redesigned the form-factor of the tiles, adopting a distinctive triangular shape, and tested new versions and materials in different conditions: wet, dry, indoor, outdoor, but also winning permission to do that in high-profile locations – New York, Paris and Brazil – which attracted interest and media coverage. As he continued to experiment and talk passionately about the potential of the technology, he was also attracting interest and new investment. He was building a business model, generating both kinetic energies as well as rich data from footfall, patenting that innovation, and doing this consistently and deliberately in the public eye.

Husqvarna Group have recently experimented with a city-centre tool hire solution called the "Battery Box" – an unattended container with 30 electronic lockers that store battery-powered garden care products. Customers can access these via a phone app to reserve tools, pay and open the locker to pick up their pre-booked power tools. The team were excited about their experiment, though there was some hesitancy about promoting or scaling the initial single Battery Box site. But Kemball-Cook's challenge was clear: if you are innovating and experimenting, do not be afraid to do it in plain sight. Make experimentation visible and intriguing, and learn from others' feedback as well your own insights. Rather than ship the product, Kemball-Cook consistently used opportunities to explore, try, test, learn and refine.

The Battery Box was just one of numerous innovations and ideas being pursued in different parts of Husqvarna Group, though Wärn and his team wanted to find ways to accelerate and crystalise these opportunities. Much of the Group were wrestling with a major transition from "Petrol to Battery", and more senior leadership thought and time were needed considering the implications of future change for products and services. The business had an active innovation platform, led across engineering, product design, as well new concept and customer insight teams.

Experimentation was used as a cornerstone of the learning design for the Husqvarna Group Future Executive Programme, with a specific series of sessions and workshops. These were led by Jules Goddard and Andrew MacLennan, and the participants were taken through the conceptual thinking and key elements of an experimentation process. Goddard hosted the group at the inspiring setting of The Design Museum in Kensington, London. MacLennan walked them through a best practice "six step" model for experimentation and pressed the group to think hard about the real business challenges, or problems, experiments might help to resolve. Four experiment groups — each with participants from different countries, functions and business units, and with different skills — were formed. The groups were given wide license by Per and Leigh to be imaginative and ambitious in their experiments. They had eight weeks to design, execute and review the outcome of their experiments, while making sure stakeholders were aware of the process. Since few were based in the same location or business unit, they also needed to keep connected with one another, managing the experiments as a group across different time zones.

This is where the importance of glue comes to the fore. It would be easy to let the process slide. After the high of being together, with Kai Wärn and members of his Executive team in London, it would be easy for the energy levels and engagement of the cohort groups to drop. There was a two-month gap between the two modules of the programme and, unlike an agreed project mandate, the nature of experiments is deliberately loose and self-determined. As such, energy levels can dip, the distraction of "business as usual" can quickly dominate, and other priorities take precedence.

Each of the experiment groups presented back their experiments and findings when they returned to London for the second part of the programme. It would be impossible here to do justice to the thoughtfulness and insights that were played back, and the imagination and creativity with which the experimentation process had been applied to real challenges within the business. There were many smart ideas, though one experiment group in particular struck a chord: an idea to develop a brand-new garden product called "spears", accelerating the design, market testing and product assembly process through a series of small experiments to test and build confidence in consumer demand for the new proposition. The group posted their concept of "spears" online to generate feedback from passionate gardeners. The feedback was positive, and the experiment team even had calls from customers (retail buyers) who wanted to know why they had launched a new product category without offering them to list it.

The executive development programme with the Husqvarna Group was memorable in many ways. Although just one of many customised executive learning programmes that London Business School is invited to design, curate and host, it was particularly well briefed by a CEO genuinely interested in the development of future talent and anchored very closely by Leigh Dagberg and Per Ericson. Wärn produced a short briefing for the cohort, which was filmed, and his leadership team spent time before, during and after the programme with the cohort members. Additionally, he held one of his regular executive management meetings in London to coincide with the programme. He hosted dinner with the group, and many of the executives from the business units attended a parallel workshop on experimentation and digital innovation. In the following autumn, the members of the programme were invited by Wärn to design and produce the businesses' annual senior management meeting, for 150 managers from around the world. Husqvarna Group clearly have a healthy combination of seasoned senior executives and emerging future leaders genuinely interested and proactive about the creation of new ideas.

Torches, torches

Three years later, in the gloomy days of late 2020 amidst the continued Covid-19 restrictions in the UK and much of the world, I was frustratedly still working from home. A parcel delivery was not a surprise, but the size and shape seemed unusual, and it was certainly not something my wife or I had ordered. The sender was from Gardena, in Germany. We unpacked the box and assembled the items. The box contained a set of decorative garden furniture, called ClickUp![12] The best way to describe it would be an elegantly crafted set of "spears", with detachable heads for water, plants, bird-feeding and, best of all, gas-lit torches. The different elements can be attached via a smart "one-click" fastening, then easily changed to match spring, summer, autumn and winter. We set the ClickUp! handles with their torch attachments in the garden that evening and watched them illuminate the autumnal gloom. A letter accompanied the gift from Tobias Koerner, Vice President Global Sales, reminding me that he had attended the LBS programme in London, and he shared again the details of the experiment, product development story and the planned launch of the new product line.

ClickUp! is available to buy from Gardena, one of the Husqvarna Group companies, born out of an idea tested during the experimentation process at LBS.[13]

The team's early experiment had helpfully galvanised confidence around the product idea with the broader division mobilised to make the innovation come to life as a real product. A form of glue had galvanised the required resources in R&D, supply chain and marketing investment along with other areas to push through and test if the experiment could be scaled and brought to life. Strategically, it shaped a new category for Husqvarna Group's Gardena division and became the entry into the area of garden decoration.

Configured for success

As mentioned earlier, experiments form a particularly useful way to get unconnected colleagues to collaborate in smart and productive ways. There are numerous examples of costs saved, ideas created, initiatives launched and funded, and real value created as an outcome of well-run experiments. My own experimentation experience is limited to a few companies and guiding a few hundred executives through the process. Not every experiment turns into a global line of modular garden furniture, but my colleagues at LBS and others can attest to thousands of experiments and the huge value of the insights they have delivered.

But it seems that the real value of experiments is in the glue they can create. The format and process of experimentation is a very particular configuration that produces "organisational advantage" through connecting disparate parts of the firm around innovation-led meaningful collaboration opportunities. They create new intellectual capital, but also stronger bonds between people. The feedback from participants is different from the typical commentary received after involvement in a team building or a mandated project team exercise.

When a senior team say that they want to get people to work together on an important project, that might be worthy, but it is very different from asking talented people to collaborate on an experiment. There is something about the sudden space, the unexpected looseness and ambiguity about outcomes, that lights up the imagination. There is something powerful given in the clear senior sponsorship of experiments, making insight generation important and serious. There is something about the stories which experiments generate that makes work seem somehow exciting and remarkable again.

There is something about experiments that creates and nurtures glue.

Applying glue

- Who owns, or drives, innovation in your firm?
- The Amazon recommendation story, as told by Gary Hamel, seems surprising. Why is that?
- How would a programme of "fail-fast-learn" experiments work in your organisation?
- See the Resources section for more best practice on leading business experiments.

Notes and references

1 The Management Innovation Lab, or MLab, was founded by Professors Julian Birkinshaw and Gary Hamel following research into sources of competitive advantage.

2 Birkinshaw, Julian. (3 May 2017) London Business School article: "Why Best Ideas Can Come From Outside the Business; How Roche Discovers New Healthcare Innovations." See: https://www.london.edu/think/diie-healthcare-innovations

3 James, R. and Goddard, J. (2021) *Business Experimentation: A Practical Guide for Driving Innovation and Performance in your Business*. Kogan Page. Written by two of the leading exponents of business experimentation and based upon their work with a variety of leading organisations, the book is comprehensive and practical in its cover of the process from problem identification, hypothesis, planning, design and analysis of experiments.

4 Sourced from a briefing note for an executive education client at LBS on the value of experimentation by Dr Andrew MacLennan. 2018. MacLennan helpfully defines an experiment as "a systematic procedure designed to discover (or illustrate) facts through observing effects." See also: https://www.andrewmaclennan.com/what-is-management-experimentation/

5 Ibid.

6 James, R. and Goddard, J. (2021) op. cit., p. 22.

7 Included in a briefing note for an executive education client at LBS on the value of experimentation; the exact company and outcome is not specified, but the hypothesis seemed intriguing and provocative.

8 The story about Greg Linden was recounted at a conference by Gary Hamel. Retrieved and transcribed from You Tube; the same story is also included in his book, co-written with Michele Zanini (2020) *Humanocracy: Creating Organisations As Amazing As The People Inside Them,* HBR Press, p. 203. Hamel notes the eventual outcome of Linden's experiment: "Today, roughly 35 percent of Amazon's retail sales are generated by site recommendations."

9 Husqvarna Group can trace its origins to its founding near the town of Husqvarna in Sweden in 1689. The company started life as a maker of muskets, and the Husqvarna logo still depicts a gun sight viewed from the end of the barrel. As with many motorcycle manufacturers, Husqvarna first began producing bicycles in the late 19th century. For more on this fascinating innovative business, with over 300 years of invention, see www.husqvarna.com/us/discover/history/

10 From the author's interview with Kai Warn. (January 2017)

11 Pavegen Systems was founded in 2009 by Laurence Kemball-Cook. Cook is a graduate from Loughborough University (in the UK), who created an innovation using footfall as a potential power source. The company he founded has gone on to manage 200 projects in 37 different countries. Source: https://www.pavegen.com/

12 ClickUp is a product of Gardena, part of the Husqvarna Group. Sourced from: https://www.gardena.com/uk/products/soil-ground/garden-decoration/clickup-handle/970496801/

13 Email from Tobias Koerner, VP Global Sales at Gardena.

8

BARRIERS TO GLUE

Hybrid working, individualisation, siloed organisations, and employee disengagement make it harder to create and cultivate glue. Ensuring autonomy, belonging and competence is key.

Creating glue has always been a significant task, requiring huge amounts of time, energy, and leadership commitment. Unfortunately, all the evidence is that creating glue is not going to get any easier. Hybrid working, remote working, individualisation, siloed organisations, changing generational preferences, and employee disengagement are all trends that are making it harder to create and cultivate glue.

The death of the office

As the world gradually began to reopen in early 2022 following the pandemic disruption of the previous two years, companies around the world were wrestling with a difficult policy conundrum. Should they require

DOI: 10.4324/9781003410690-9

employees to return to the office, encourage them to return but not require that attendance, or allow continued flexibility? In May, the CEO of Twitter, Parag Agrawal, confirmed that the remote working policy introduced by his predecessor would remain and "employees can work from home 'forever', or 'wherever you feel most productive and creative'."[1] For a technology company this did not seem a surprise, and Google and Meta followed suit, though their Silicon Valley neighbours Apple were requiring a more hybrid approach. By the end of 2022, Twitter would have a new CEO and a complete 180-degree reversal of Agrawal's freedom pass, but by then many other tech and professional firms had embraced the flexibility trend.

Apple CEO Tim Cook took a different approach and told staff that they should work three days a week from the company's US$5 billion-dollar mega-headquarters in Cupertino, California. In a note to staff Cook said:

> For all that we've been able to achieve while many of us have been separated, the truth is that there has been something essential missing from this past year: each other.[2]

Unusually for Apple, an internal row became public as some staff protested over the company's demands, but Cook's view remained unchanged that video calls could not replace the experience of working together. On Wall Street, Jamie Dimon, Head of J.P.Morgan (the biggest bank in the US), took a dim view of homeworking: "It doesn't work for those who want to hustle. It doesn't work for spontaneous idea generation. It doesn't work for culture."[3]

Morgan Stanley chief executive James Gorman, aghast at his empty office amidst a resurgent dining scene in New York said: "If you can go into a restaurant in New York City, you can come into the office."[4]

In June 2021, the professional services firm Deloitte had made a bold move and told all its 20,000 UK employees:[5] "You can work from home forever." For many employees, Deloitte's flexible working decision was the announcement they had craved since the start of the "lockdown" restrictions in March 2020. A guaranteed commute of merely ten steps from bed to bathroom to virtual office, with all the environmental, well-being and work-life balance benefits that offered, was now assured. Deloitte's HR department had surely seized the zeitgeist and been as uber-flexible as possible in their policy response to an employee preference for homeworking. Deloitte were understandably keen to be seen as an enlightened and progressive employer, enabling a more mature, flexible relationship with its staff. The Partners at Deloitte, having worked for over a decade to secure a corner office, now faced the prospect of gazing out through frosted glass onto a deserted vacuous open-plan floor. There was now little point in commuting from the leafy suburbs. How their newly hired trainees (Deloitte is one of the biggest graduate recruiters in the UK), experienced hires and intra-firm movers would be able to get a sense of team, tone and culture of the place seemed less of a concern. At firms like Deloitte, the future of work would be, going forward, flexed around the preferences of the individual.

Whilst many cheered Deloitte's announcement, the consequences may not be wholly beneficial and, as Microsoft found from surveying their own people around the world, their managers and employees saw the performance impact of remote working very differently. How large swathes of staff will be able to get the value of close collaborative working, and the serendipity of random conversations, and the simple shared humanity of working in proximity to others, remains an open question. The announcement by Deloitte was also significant for the property sector, and many commentators believed that their announcement, followed by numerous other technology, financial services and professional services firms, signaled a death warrant for the office long-lease.

Deloitte's announcement seemed to suggest that the pandemic had ushered in an irreversible working revolution that would reshape our lives for years to come. But not everyone agreed. Writing in *The Times*, Sir James Dyson, the founder and chief engineer of Dyson, described the UK government's plans to go even further than Deloitte's progressive approach and make flexible working a legal entitlement for all employees as a "misguided approach [that] will generate friction between employers and employees, creating further bureaucratic drag."[6]

Meanwhile in the US, another founder saw the issue as even more fundamental, requiring a hardcore response.

Elon Musk thinks differently

After months of uncertainty about whether the deal would close, Elon Musk finally bought the social media platform Twitter on 27 October 2022.

He was filmed the previous evening walking into the Twitter offices, carrying a porcelain sink. The caption shared with his followers read: "Entering Twitter HQ – Let that sink in". Within days, he sketched out a loose vision for the future of the platform, promising to block the spambots, protect free speech and build an "everything app". The media furore, aghast that a declared free-speech libertarian was now at the helm, was extraordinary, but Musk was undeterred. He quickly implemented changes, each one announced through Twitter itself. In his very first few days of ownership he set about a series of upgrades to the platform itself, changing verification protocols, introducing a US$8 charge for authentication, firing a large swathe of staff and bluntly ending his predecessor's policy of "you can work from home forever". Given Musk's track record as an innovator, visionary and disruptor, taking a contrarian view was no surprise, but more interesting was his rationale for the decision. For Musk it was all about productivity and he, suitably, shared his view on Twitter with his 115 million followers.

> If you look at the Tesla AI Autopilot team, it is about 150 engineers, and they're outperforming teams that they're competing against that are 3,000 engineers. I'm a big believer that a small number of exceptional people can be highly motivated and can do better than a large number of people who are pretty good and moderately motivated. That's my philosophy.[7]

Musk was being consistent, managing the technology engineers and media specialists at Twitter in the same way he had the software and hardware engineers in Tesla. Earlier in the year he had written to Tesla's staff confirming that work-from-home arrangements were "no longer acceptable" and "anyone who wishes to do remote work must be in the office for a minimum (and I mean minimum) of 40 hours per week or depart Tesla. This is less than we ask of factory workers".[8]

The contrast with dominant market trend towards greater flexibility, individual choice and remote working could not have been starker, and he wrote to the employees at Twitter to explain why he had made the change: "I am a big believer in the esprit de corps and effectiveness of being physically in the same location."[9] Musk's communication landed shortly after the release of a viral video from a Twitter employee called

"Rachel Kurivila" (her handle; perhaps not her real name) offering a glimpse of a typical day at the Twitter office,[10] showing it sparsely populated with employees, enjoying a spa-like environment dedicated to meditation, exercise, fresh food, ice-tea consumption and relaxation. The coincidence is probably no more than that, but on 16 November 2022 Musk sent a memo to all staff at Twitter requiring them to sign-up to a new "hardcore" requirement of long hours and high intensity or leave with three months' severance. The memo, headed "Fork in the Road", is probably one of the most succinct and provocative counter-expressions against the modern trend of employee-centric flexibility and workplace well-being support. Musk cancelled the free in-house catering and sent his incendiary memo.

> Going forward, to build a breakthrough Twitter 2.0 and succeed in an increasingly competitive world, we will need to be extremely hardcore. This will mean working long hours at high intensity. Only exceptional performance will constitute a passing grade. Twitter will also be much more engineering driven. Design and product management will still be very important and report to me, but those writing great code will constitute the majority of our team and have the greatest sway. If you are sure that you want to be part of the new Twitter, please click yes on the link below. Anyone who has not done so by 5pm ET tomorrow (Thursday) will receive three months of severance. Whatever decision you make, thank you for your efforts to make Twitter successful. Elon.[11]

The subsequent news coverage varied wildly, though CNBC confidently reported some three-quarters of Twitter's 7,500 staff left the firm in aftermath of Musk's new "hardcore" approach. How things will play out for Musk and his Twitter transformation is uncertain. What is more predictable is that this is a corporate drama that will play out in the most public way imaginable. Musk has placed himself both philosophically and culturally as a counterbalance to the prevailing employee-centric trends, with a clear sense, from experience, that what worked so well for electric car production and space transportation is the right model for a San Francisco-based progressive social media company. As with the Partners at Deloitte, he has made a big call and taken a position. In time, each may come to regret that certitude, or in time, they may be lauded for it.

A eulogy for the office

Musk is clearly a fan of the office, but the office is not often included as one of humanity's greatest achievements. The office's reputation is unfashionable at best and often associated as a dull burdensome context for our working lives. We take great joy in recognising the cringe-worthy reality of TV shows like *The Office*, *Corporate*, or *IT Crowd*. It is, though, possible to make the case for an alternative view of the office. Historians can have their reach of the Roman Empire, the wonder of the pyramids at Giza, and the written Constitution of the United States. Scientists can have their sequenced DNA, the discovery of Penicillin, landing space-rockets on the Moon and breakthrough medicines. Engineers can swoon at the Hoover Dam, the Great Wall of China, or the new Shrewsbury bypass (in the UK). But for the world of business, the modern office, in many ways, encompasses the zenith of management achievement in the past 200 years. Unlike the Lunar Module, Blockbuster Videos, or Florence Nightingale's lamp, perhaps the office is not bound for the museum and forms an essential platform for organisations to reside in, grow and develop. Perhaps the single best expression of a company culture and how it values its people's collective energies is the workplace it provides for its staff.

The writer Simon Sinek wrote memorably: "Corporate culture matters. How management chooses to treat its people impacts everything – for better or for worse."[12] The single best embodiment and forum for that culture remains the workplace. In 1854, when Sir Titus Salt, in the village of Saltaire, Yorkshire, decided to build an enormous new factory alongside the canal,[13] he also built well-appointed, decent sanitary housing for his workers within yards of the mill. Two hundred years before our current debate about remote and in-person working, he found a different, more humane, way to kill the commute. For him, where his people worked, were educated, socialised and lived was all part and parcel of the same endeavour. Today, we may not live on-site or so literally "above the shop", but our workplaces still define something of who we are socially, professionally, organisationally. In part this is because the workplace is not the same as home. The former *Financial Times* business columnist (and in a second career as a secondary school mathematics teacher) Lucy Kellaway[14] recently wrote a love letter to the office in the FT.

The office helps keep us sane . . . First, it imposes routine, without which most of us fall to pieces. Even better, it creates a barrier between work and home. On arrival we escape the chaos (or monotony) of our hearths; better still, we escape from our usual selves.[15]

Great modern workplaces, at their best, are designed with a level of architectural, creative, artistic and sociological intent, built on foundations of profound learning and shared best practice from around the world. Architects, developers and designers have crafted extraordinary spaces for serendipity, collaboration, openness, transparency, democracy, hierarchy, status, drama and theatre. If you spend some time in a great office, like Apple Park in Silicon Valley, the Hearst Tower offices in Manhattan, Linked-in in San Francisco or the very best-appointed offices in London of UBS, Deutsche Bank, Clifford Chance, Barclays, McKinsey, Rio Tinto or BP, you cannot help but be inspired, awed and energized. Perhaps you might even want to give more of yourself for an organisation that gifts you that working environment and affords such close proximity to others similarly motivated to be there with you. In a hybrid working world where the future of the office is seen by some commentators to be tenuous at best, a property developer, their lessee or the firm planning a relocation needs a profoundly good rationale for going ahead. Some corporate leaders have clear confidence in the future of the office. A few more recent examples in London are notable in their thoughtful design and particularly their purpose.

Bloomberg

Bloomberg's European headquarters was opened by its founder in 2017, signalling a much-needed vote of confidence in the UK and the City amidst uncertainty about the UK's departure from the European Union. Designed by Sir Norman Forster, it was opened with much fanfare: "The first wholly owned and designed Bloomberg building in the world, it is designed to facilitate collaboration and fuel innovation, and will bring Bloomberg's 4,000 London-based employees under one roof for the first time."[16] It is a stunning working environment and notably, it fits the organisation's convictions with unrivalled sustainability credentials in its construction, design, and operation.

Sky

The upgrading of Sky's company headquarters in 2016 allowed Sky, guided by its architect Amanda Lavette, to recalibrate the way staff collaborate and organise their work time at the round-the-clock broadcaster. The workplace design breaks down divisions between staff, whilst avoiding some of the alienating and productivity-sapping dangers of hot-desking workplaces. Some 3,500 employees work across 20 zones with six restaurants. Jeremy Darroch, Sky's chief executive at the time of the opening, said that the vast scale of the operations raised a critical design question: "Do you build multiple buildings or one big building?"[17] Sky chose the latter, as multiple buildings mean that people tend to stay inside "their" own building and mingle less. In the Sky campus, you can walk through the whole organisation, though it will take ten minutes to walk across from one side to the other! Sky wanted an open building where, for example, finance, marketing, presenting and operations staff could meet and mingle, and see one another at work. The workspace is bright and airy, and the building's steel staircases appear to be randomly scattered, though this again a deliberate design feature to encourage people to circulate and mix.

Apple and Google

Post-pandemic, the trend continues with a resurgence of the corporate office, or campus, or hub or home, as they are increasingly badged, continuing apace. In late 2022 Google's new campus in Kings Cross, London, was being topped out. A brand-new design by Thomas Heatherwick, it is a 14-storey, one million square foot "landscaper" and is due to fully open in 2024. The first Google-owned and designed building outside the US,[18] it will be the working "home" to 4,000 staff, taking advantage of amenities including a 25-metre swimming pool on the ninth floor, outdoor parks and running tracks, and a multi-use games area, where "Googlers" will be able to play basketball, five-a-side football or tennis. Meanwhile, south of the River Thames, Apple is fitting out its new mega-headquarters as part of the multi-billion-dollar Battersea Power Station redevelopment.[19]

No work-from-home "minimalist Zoom set-up" (even from a cool garden cabin office) can compete with an environment designed with the vision and imagination of an accomplished architect and interior space designer. If your organisation does not have a thoughtfully designed modern workplace for your people, this sends signals to prospective hires and current staff about your firm's future ambition, values and strategy. The reason for this is that whatever the advancement of remote connectivity, or video technology, the shared workplace is one of the clearest ways in which an organisation manifests its employee proposition and its brand. In the 2000s, Tesco maintained a famously drab and underwhelming head office in Cheshunt, North London. The Tesco CEO, Terry Leahy, was an FTSE100 "darling" and acclaimed leader, not for the quality of artwork in his dreary head office, but for his rigorous focus on creating value for customers through cost efficiency and supplier management. But even Leahy relented to modernity, a few years later, moving the operation to a shiny modern facility in Welywn Garden City.

The new workplace

Organisations can build a greater sense of collaboration, shared ownership and positivity through the deliberate investment in a well-designed physical setting, aimed at harnessing employee productivity. The modern workplace is, by definition, a hybrid-working platform, providing connectivity to employees and other parts of the organisation as well as a way of connecting customers, suppliers and advisors. But is also serves other purposes. For Bloomberg it was "designed to facilitate collaboration and fuel innovation"; for Sky it was Darroch's need to join the whole organisation under one roof, and "recalibrate the way staff collaborate and organise their work" with staff from different divisions in plain sight and with an ease of access to one another. Google's obvious emphasis is on leisure, exercise and social connection, with employees anticipated to be in an after-work football game with one-another as much as in a team meeting with a schedule and agenda.

Apple's new HQ is deliberately placed in an iconic setting, repurposed, re-invented for the 21st century, again co-locating hundreds of teams and departments under one extraordinary new roof. The emphasis is consistent and common: connection, collaboration, shared space, encouraging contact, the happenstance of meeting, the intrigue and serendipity of seeing, hearing and better understanding what others do. These uber-expensive examples are designed to perform like working "platforms" with facilities, physically and philosophically, purposefully designed with engagement and collaboration in mind. Places where, perhaps, one hopes that glue might more easily flourish.

You do not need to have the billion-dollar investment or engage a world-famous architect. I have worked for clients based in converted barns, in light-filled roof spaces above a warehouse, in a small-scale shared workspace where one corner of the floor was heroically and proudly owned by a start-up business, and in a crowded annex building, piled high with tech and an endlessly eclectic playlist. These places had some energy and verve, even if the air-conditioning was not perfect.

The best workplaces are those that are designed with employees as stakeholders and contributors to the design process. Your workplace design should be a thoughtful mix of virtual, with a better-equipped, more purposeful office, studio, campus or workshop. The critical point about workplace is that you must give a reason for employees to take pride not just in their work but also in their place. If the only point to the commute is to arrive at an office and reconnect with colleagues still working remotely, then the place becomes pointless. If you get that shared workplace right, your corporate "home" as enjoyed, explored and used by your employees, can be a great expression of shared culture; a physical manifestation of how you think about and value employees and, in that, whether you care more of less for creating glue.

The death of the office may have been a little prematurely predicted, and a renaissance in smart thinking about the role, function and value of the corporate workspace is alive and well. A purposeful design of working and collaborating should be something leadership teams need to attend to with as much thought and attention as the HR "policy" guidance about homeworking, flexibility and office attendance. Whatever the outcome of that debate, the best workplaces are still designed as a shared valuable resource for collaboration and can be a source of pride, as part of an employee proposition that embraces people, not simply contracts with them from a distance. (See Figure 8.1 and Chapter 10 on Organisational Glue for more on this obligation to embrace.) You do not need to go as far as Musk's "fork in the road" ultimatum but, in the near term, as much intellectual capital and leadership imagination should be applied to encouraging employees to attend the office as has been given to allowing them to stay away.

Employee proposition

Contracting	Embracing
Decentralised, remote and hybrid working predominates, with little regular office attendance (which remains popular with employees).	An emphasis on the firm's workplace, as a valued resource, a collaboration venue and a source of pride. Flexibility varies, with office attendance encouraged.
Employee benefits and policy generously shaped around all individuals, with conditions and reward determined by market-rates.	Employee benefits, flexible working policy and reward are shaped by the service and collaborative needs of the firm, as they best serve the customer.
"Employees" are variously employed, contracted, temporary or consulting for the firm, with large variances in terms, conditions.	The majority of employees are employed directly by the firm, with broad participation in variable reward or the firm's share scheme.
Control and procedures dominate, with approvals needed for trivial matters and risk aversion common.	An environment of psychological safety, where employees feel able to try new things, experiment and take the initiative.

Figure 8.1 The firm's employee proposition is one that seeks to embrace

Motivating employees to give more

Where you physically work and with whom is important, but whatever the state of your office, the economy or the disruption felt, the key employee engagement question remains, since the industrial revolution and before: "Show me the money."[20] Most corporate organisations rely on a pretty-well worn, tried-and-tested toolkit of incentives to retain, engage and motivate their employees. Each year, leadership teams and their HR departments, hunker down and agonise over annual pay awards, discretionary bonus schemes, employee benefits (including health and well-being schemes), flexible working arrangements, transport policies and other aspects of the renumeration package. The overall reward proposition, sometimes called a "basket", is incrementally tweaked and enhanced at the margins, or even revised, with elements withdrawn, when the business environment changes.

Essentially, all the reward levers are the employer's own; any motivational differential is extrinsically sought by the firm. In other words, employers expect that employees are motivated to perform by the mixture and value of rewards on offer. For some, there may be other elements to the motivation mix, such as opportunities for progression, additional development and the chance of high-profile assignments. But, more often, organisations fall back on the old maxim that incentives drive behaviour. There is nothing new in this, and the familiar tension it creates is a recipe for endless hours of debate amongst management teams. In non-unionised environments, or for the reward of senior employees, the debates are perhaps less involved or formal, but essentially the relationship and power-balance is the same between the employer and the employee.

In recent years this reliance on incentives to drive "extrinsic" motivation as the only way of getting the best out of people has begun to be questioned. We have seen the emergence of businesses which emphasise their purpose, social convictions, societal goals or environmental credentials as the way of attracting, retaining and motivating talent. The employer/employee contract is more nuanced, with moral, values-driven and socially conscious criteria affecting that relationship. A new employee may know that they may not get paid as much working at your firm as they would at the more established company up the road, but they will also know that they will not be polluting the oceans.

The neatest way I have seen this different approach described is in a fabulous book by Simon Sinek, called *Start With Why*.[21] Writing about consumer behaviour, Sinek argues that people don't buy what you do, but why you do it. In an open employment market, that dictum holds true, people will want to work for you, not because of what you do but why you do it. Talent is engaged and motivated by your underlying purpose as an organisation. Desires and needs can be met by a different, non-monetary, kind of reward. But there are also desires and needs – even more fundamental than these – that increasingly need to be considered.

Autonomy, belonging and competence: As simple as ABC

A fascinating theory called Self-Determination Theory (SDT), developed by Edward Deci and Richard Ryan,[22] emphasises the importance of intrinsic motivation. Managers and leaders, need to properly understand their organisations as social environments required to satisfy the basic psychological needs of their employees. As we all know and have experienced, the long-standing motivational philosophy and practice of business is based on the dominant belief that the best way to get people to perform tasks is to prompt, or reinforce, their behaviour with incentives and rewards. I worked in the City of London for over a decade and the annual performance bonus cycle, which dominated all thought and behaviours for a large part of the year, was one of the most extraordinary psychological ploys ever devised. Self-Determination Theory proposes a different way of drawing motivation and in a way that ought to be music to the glue-creating leader.

SDT proposes that all human beings have three basic psychological needs that are innate and universal.[23] These are needs for autonomy, relatedness (or belonging) and competence. Satisfaction of these basic needs promotes the optimal motivational traits and states of autonomous motivation and intrinsic aspiration, which facilitate psychological health and effective engagement with the world. Those "universal needs" are worth restating and thinking about in a work context.

There are three key human needs in Self-Determination Theory, listed below and shown in Figure 8.2.

- **Autonomy** – the ability to make choice and a desire to control one's own actions and outcomes.
- **Relatedness** or "belonging" – the importance of relating to other people, and a desire for close relationships, to feel part of a group.
- **Competence** – which is being able to use strengths and a desire to develop new strengths and capabilities.

Self-Determination Theory

Autonomy

People need to feel in control of their goals. This sense of being able to take personal action, that will result in real change, plays a major part in helping people feel self-determined.

Belonging

People need to experience a sense of relatedness and connection to other people. Feelings of belonging are enhanced when people are respected and cared for by others and they can reciprocate.

Competence

People need to gain mastery of tasks and learn different skills. When people feel that they are equipped for success, they are more likely to take actions that will help them achieve their goals.

Figure 8.2 ABC model adapted from the work of Edward Deci and Richard Ryan[24]

If truly "universal", then these basic psychological needs also apply to each of us within the workplace, and since we spend so much of our adult lives there, understanding and "tapping" these needs is crucial to ensure that the environment created is not just safe, in a health and safety or a psychological sense, but is one in which people's needs are met and they are made able to thrive.

The goal of the glue-focused leader is to nurture a powerful dynamic between highly engaged talented people, enabling the organisation to grow and thrive. To do this and satisfy their psychological needs, leaders need to work hard to give their people autonomy, encourage a deeper sense of belonging, through strong relationships, and to enable them to apply and develop their talents or "competencies". Deci and Ryan have confirmed autonomy, belonging and competence as basic psychological needs, but in proactively satisfying these needs, leaders can also create glue.

Freedom in the frame

It is reassuring when a counter-intuitive theory like this is borne out by real-world experience, where you discover that greater autonomy does drive real commitment, competencies and potential can be fully realized, and a greater sense of belonging can be built. Too many leaders feel they have to control and closely manage, without allowing space for their best people to flourish.

In late 2011, I was given an opportunity to join the global marketing leadership team of HSBC, reporting to Chris Clark, the Group Head of Marketing. Chris had joined HSBC as its Head of Brand Strategy in 2001 from advertising agency Saatchi and Saatchi and, after a number of roles in marketing and customer experience, he was appointed to the top marketing job reporting to the Group CEO. His was one of the biggest professional marketing jobs of its type – certainly in the financial services sector – steering the global HSBC unified brand, guiding campaigns and customer insight across nearly 100 countries and territories around the world. I recall the guestimate at the time was that Chris would have responsibility for over a thousand marketers spending more than a billion US dollars each year.

I had met him a few years earlier, as he was a regular guest speaker on the global induction programme that Clive Bannister had launched in private banking. He would fly from London to Geneva, speak to all the new hires, catch up with the local business CEO, and fly back that evening to Canary Wharf, without fuss or ceremony. Before I had ever heard of the phrase, Chris was an exemplar manager who provided his senior team with what I now know of as "freedom in the frame".[25] The size and responsibility of his role was enormous by any standards, and the matrix nature of the global function was complex, with competing country, regional and global priorities, as well as rigorous compliance standards, for brand, creative and sponsorship assets. But he managed this by allowing enormous degrees of autonomy to his top team – and implicitly to their teams, so they could get on and execute good work. His management style was not one through supervision, but one of providing access. He was available 24/7 every day across the year to his team across the world, able to help, clarify, confirm or reject ideas and, when not needed, he allowed autonomy to his team so they could be ambitious, creative and imaginative. His monthly senior management meetings were all about creating a forum for creative inputs and ideas. He hired a strong COO, who made sure the numbers added up, the processes were robust and the function was not sloppy, but his personal focus was "the work" (campaigns, creative, partnerships) and the people. He personally shouldered much of the heavyweight politics and negotiations within the head office, so his team had air cover when needed. When he organised a global get together for all the senior marketers around the world, he gave smart talented people the latitude to shape the agenda and contribute, so the spotlight was more widely shared, encouraging and promoting great colleagues like Andrea de Vincentiis, Suresh Balaji, Helen Westbrook, Jennifer Ting and Tricia Weener. HSBC is not renowned as an organisation where such freedom might thrive. In my time there, Chris's leadership style was not typical, with most managers relying on multiple layers of control, reporting, oversight and second-guessing. Here, like Joe Garner (mentioned in Chapter 5), was another "unusual" manager: an exceptional glue-creating leader.

Existentialist cultures

The idea that your best people will thrive on autonomy has a longer history than Deci and Ryan's relatively recent proposition. In 1978, Charles Handy[26] developed his theory of the Four Types of Culture and published them in his book *Gods of Management*.[27] He classified four distinct management cultures, using the ancient Greek gods to symbolise each: a Club culture (Zeus); Role culture (Apollo); Task culture (Athena); and an Existential culture (Dionysus). All of these cultures are wonderfully conceived and described, and Handy proposes that all four can co-exist within the same organisation. Some 50 years ago, and long before digital platforms, remote and hybrid working, he seemed able to anticipate the exact mode in which many of us wish to work today. He described an existential culture as full of expert professionals and talented performers, connected by a higher purpose, where personal freedom and flexible work is the foundation for success.

> Here, individuals' talent and skills are the organization's greatest assets. The existentialist culture is best for organizations that depend entirely on the talent or skill of expert professionals and "star" performers. For example, virtual companies that employ a diverse mix of contractors and employees are often existentialist. Many start-ups and partnerships also adopt an existentialist culture. This culture is a good fit when your organization needs to attract the best talent possible, or when you work within a group of equals, such as a partnership. Personal freedom is the foundation of an existentialist culture. So give your team members the autonomy that they need to do their jobs as they see fit. If possible, allow them to work from home or to set their own schedule. You just might find that if you take a step back, their engagement and productivity will improve.[28]

Experiments provide autonomy

So how might you test this belief that "stepping back" actually improves engagement and productivity? I described earlier that experiments were a way of letting talented people off the leash. Experiment groups are by definition afforded great autonomy, to roam, to wander and to wonder, to hypothesise and try out ideas, without fear of failure. They are exercises that can help leaders make better decisions about strategy, but they are also inherently exercises that allow participants to self-determine the area of focus, the topic, to hypothesis, the methods used and the way it will be debriefed. Jules Goddard[29] beautifully describes the way this freedom and autonomy energises people.

Smart people do not respond positively to processes and systems that emphasise alignment, conformity, and aversion to risk. They wanted to be trusted to exercise their talents in their own way. What they want and need most from their leaders is to be able to express their talents, develop their expertise, to be freed from administrative distractions and to be allowed to fail, to be recognised for their expertise, and to have time to pursue private efforts.[30]

Experiments may not fill all of this employer-employee deficit, but they do go a long way to providing some space and freedom to be found and the need for autonomy can be met.

Experiments connect teams in a collaborative effort, helping dispersed team members connect and build relationships with others. If part of a learning development programme (like the example shared in Chapter 2 about the HPDP cohort in China, or the Husqvarna experiment groups in Chapter 7), then very close bonds are created over time, not through the happenstance of work, but through the very deliberate configuration and choices made in determining those participating on the programmes, and those working together on experiments. It is this sense of esprit de corps that engenders more than just a task-force but a sense of belonging. Experiment groups often embrace this, adopting quirky names for their experiment groups, or NASA-style mission names for the experiments themselves, launching Gazebo, or Spears, or Bling or SuperQ! Without a penny being spent, experiment groups seem to inculcate a sense of relatedness to one another amongst participants, and that all important need of belonging is found.

Intergenerational differences

Work was disrupted during the lockdown and workplace restrictions adopted by authorities during the Covid-19 pandemic. But that disruption did not end with the lifting of restrictions; it precipitated a wave of change affecting perceptions about work-life balance, commuting, home-working and some exhaustion from "always on" Zoom fatigue.

Where you work was not just the only issue, but whether you returned to work at all. In 2021 employees around the world quit their jobs in record numbers,[31] some 43 million leaving their jobs in the USA. The Great Resignation,[32] a term coined in May 2021, describes the record number of people leaving their jobs since the beginning of the pandemic. After an extended period of working from home with no commute, many people decided their work-life balance was more important to them and that the rewards no longer made sense. This revolution in the world of work appears to set to continue with PWC's Global Workforce Survey[33] in March 2022 finding that one in five workers globally plan to quit their jobs.

The Great Resignation makes planning difficult and absorbs managers in huge resourcing efforts. But whilst busy scrambling to respond tactically and keep the business running as a senior business manager, what else can you do? The key question in the "war for talent" used to be how you could answer: "Why should I work for you?" Now, amidst the disruption of the Great Resignation, the big people challenge that needs answering is: "Why should I bother staying?"

Another report[34] in 2021 by PWC delves deep into the mindset of millennials (defined by PWC as employees aged 31 and under) and perhaps provides some clues to the root causes of the talent exodus. None of it bodes well. Attracting young recruits is not the issue; keeping them for long looks impossible. Some of the headlines from that report are sobering and employer loyalty is for the birds. Over a quarter of millennials now expect to have six employers or more, compared with just 10% in 2008. Of those currently working, 38% said they were actively looking for a different role and 43% said they were open to offers. Only 18% expect to stay with their current employer for the long term.

The report also points towards a connectivity gap. The millennials and younger digital natives are actively engaged and connected 24/7 to one another, but not to you (their employer). It is difficult to build meaningful relationships or a sense of belonging when remote and hybrid working is the default mode of connection. Strikingly, 41% of millennials said they prefer to communicate electronically at work rather than face to face or over the telephone.

Employers are having to quickly come to terms with the differing inter-generational preferences between those born in the last century and those now cutting their early career teeth. These differences seem more profound than just fashion sense and digital nativism, but they may also have something more fundamental in common than the differences the

PWC report suggests. Lynda Gratton, a world-renowned expert on human resources and culture, warns against relying on biased or over-generalised distinctions based on age and to instead think more about the common humanity that runs through each generation.

> Whilst much loved by marketing and branding, these descriptions have very limited validity and are often simply stereotypes. They implicitly assume that everyone within a generation has similar hopes and aspirations, and that generations are very different from each other. It turns out there is both more diversity within a generation, and more that unites across generations. Whatever our age, we all had to find our identity as we grew up, struggled to find a partner, felt concerned about the world we grew up in, wanted the best for our children, hoped we would make a positive difference. These are the life events that unite us.[35]

Bridging the gap

Some firms are tackling the generation gap by finding a forum to better understand perspectives both ways. Canary Wharf Group, the developer and landlord of a huge estate in the east of London, took the innovative step in March 2022 of appointing its first "next generation" Junior Board. Sponsored by the CEO, Shobi Khan, the 13 Board members were appointed to act as a sounding board and platform to generate ideas and innovation to help shape the future direction of the business. The Board members have a diverse range of experiences representing different backgrounds and aspects of the business. Jane Hollinshead, of Canary Wharf Group, described it as a way of listening and learning.

> Listening to and learning from our next generation of talent is a fundamental to our culture and our future success. It is important for us to be exposed to new and different perspectives as well as developing and nurturing the talent of our workforce as we continue to move forward in our strategic objectives.[36]

If you are looking to keep younger and older employees, the vibes and tides are against you, and if you are looking to attract and retain new talent, it is an exhausting time to be a people manager. The economic currents and the cost of living in many countries may wash back against these tides, making exit rates slow down and younger employees more circumspect about hopping around. But the age-old challenge remains for organisations: not just to attract and retain people, but to make working meaningful, at times inspiring, and to develop a sense of belonging. To stretch our glue idea further, firms need to be places where people want to stick around.

Applying glue

- What are the ways in which you can encourage Autonomy, develop a sense of Belonging and allow your people to use their full Competence, and feel stretched as well?
- Arrange to visit other workplaces (customers, constants, recruiters, suppliers). What do they do to enable collaboration, communication and fun?
- Has your workplace been intentionally designed and re-purposed for a hybrid workforce?
- How are you and your organisation finding ways to listen to the next generation of leaders?

Notes and references

1 From Forbes online. (5 March 2022) "Twitter Employees Can Work from Home 'Forever' or 'Wherever You Feel Most Productive and Creative'." Retrieved from: https://www.forbes.com/sites/jackkelly/2022/03/05/twitter-employees-can-work-from-home-forever-or-wherever-you-feel-most-productive-and-creative/

2 The Guardian. (16 August 2022) "We are excited to move forward with the pilot and believe that this revised framework will enhance our ability to work flexibly, while preserving the in-person collaboration that is so essential to our culture," Cook said in the memo. The quote was also reported on CNBC. Retrieved from: https://www.cnbc.com/2021/06/03/apple-employees-to-return-to-office-three-days-a-week-in-september.html

3 Reuters. (4 May 2021) "Working From Home 'Doesn't Work for Those Who Want to Hustle'. J.P.Morgan CEO." Retrieved from: https://www.reuters.com/article/us-jp-morgan-ceo-idUSKBN2CL1HQ

4 BBC News online. (15 June 2021) "If You Can Eat Out, You Can Go to the Office", Says Bank Boss." Retrieved from: https://www.bbc.co.uk/news/business-57487963

5 The Independent. (19 June 2021) "Deloitte Tells its 20,000 UK Employees They Can Work from Home Forever – Auditing Giant to Shift to Fully Flexible Working Post-pandemic." Retrieved from: https://www.independent.co.uk/life-style/deloitte-work-from-home-employees-b1868977.html. Deloitte's own press release, retrieved from: https://www2.deloitte.com/uk/en/pages/press-releases/articles/deloitte-gives-its-20000-people-the-choice-of-when-and-where-they-work.html. Deloitte's employee research revealed that "96% of Deloitte's people want to have the freedom to choose how flexibly they will work in the future".

6 The Times. (8 December 2022) "UK's Competitiveness is Turning to Dust Under Flexible Working Diktat," written by James Dyson. Retrieved from: https://www.thetimes.co.uk/article/uk-s-competitiveness-is-turning-to-dust-under-flexible-working-diktat-6x6pmq03k

7 From @SawyerMerritt on Twitter. (4 November 2022) Retrieved from: https://twitter.com/sawyermerritt/status/1592023564693417984

8 Reported by CNBC. (1 June 2022) "Elon Musk tells Tesla Workers to Return to the Office Full Time or Resign." Retrieved from: https://www.cnbc.com/2022/06/01/elon-musk-reportedly-tells-tesla-workers-to-be-in-office-full-time-or-resign.html

9 Ibid.

10 Video retrieved via Blaze Media/News. (27 October 2022) "Twitter 'Day in a Life' Video Indicates Lots of Downtime, Very Little Actual Work." Retrieved from: https://www.theblaze.com/news/twitter-day-in-life-video

11 "The Fork in the Road" episode was reported by the Guardian. (16 November 2022) "Elon Musk gives Twitter staff deadline to commit to being 'hardcore': Remaining staff given until Thursday to confirm they will work 'long hours at high intensity' as part of 'the new Twitter'." Further notes: No public figures for resignations were released by Twitter following Musk's "fork in the road" ultimatum, though various media outlets (with their source "people on Twitter who claimed to have to quit Twitter") reported significant exits of between 300 (Reuters) and 1,200 (Rolling Stone). In a weird and wonderful twist to the story, two unemployed actors, using pseudonyms Rahul Ligma and Daniel Johnson, were interviewed outside Twitter HQ by major media broadcasters, claiming to be devastated at being let go by Twitter. CNBC reporter Deirdre Bosa tweeted a photo of the two men, commenting: "It's happening. Entire team of data engineers let go. These are two of them."

Later the two featured in a photoshoot with Musk, who clearly saw the funny side to the actors' publicity stunt.

12   Quote attributed to Simon Sinek from 2014, across numerous sources, though the original source has not been identified. Notably, Sinek has not objected to its attribution. Retrieved from "Your Company Culture is Everything" from Forbes online: https://www.forbes.com/sites/shephyken/2022/06/19/your-company-culture-is-everything/?sh=6dbd78b87d7f

13   History and resources about Titus Salt and Saltaire. Retrieved from: https://www.saltairecollection.org/saltaire-history/foundation-of-saltaire/

14   Lucy Kellaway OBE is a British journalist turned maths teacher who continues to write occasionally for the FT. For more, see: www.ft.com/lucy-kellaway

15   The Financial Times. (15 May 2020) "We Will Miss the Office if it Dies." Lucy Kellaway. Retrieved from: https://www.ft.com/content/6a84c3a0-9440-11ea-abcd-371e24b679ed

16   Bloomberg's own guide to the building. Retrieved from: https://www.bloomberg.com/company/offices/bloomberg-london/

17   The Financial Times. (2 May 2017) "Sky's the Limit for Latest Theory in Office Design." A revamp allowed the UK broadcaster to redefine the way staff collaborate and work. Retrieved from: https://www.ft.com/content/2d895f0c-1acb-11e7-a266-12672483791a

18   The Metro (19 April 2022) Retrieved from: https://metro.co.uk/2022/04/19/googles-massive-kings-cross-hq-will-span-11-floors-and-1000000-sq-ft-16494552/?ito=article.desktop.share.top.link

19   Battersea PowerStation development. Retrieved from: https://batterseapowerstation.co.uk/

20   From the 1996 film *Jerry Maguire* directed by Cameron Crowe and starring Tom Cruise as Jerry. Football player Rod Tidwell (Cuba Gooding, Jr.) isn't thrilled with Jerry's performance as his agent, and he has a simple way for Jerry to convince him to stay: "Show me the money."

21   Sinek, S. (2011) *Start With Why*. Penguin Books.

22   Deci and Ryan developed the Self-Determination Theory of Motivation, toppling the dominant belief that the best way to get human beings to perform tasks is to reinforce their behaviour with rewards. Edward Deci is a Professor of Psychology and Social Sciences at the University of Rochester (New York) in the United States, and the director of his research programmes on human motivation. Richard Ryan is a professor at the Institute for Psychology and Education at the Australian Catholic University and a research professor at the University of Rochester, New York.

23   See article from the American Psychological Association titled, "The Intrinsic Motivation of Richard Ryan and Edward Deci", which is a useful summary of

their work at: https://www.apa.org/members/content/intrinsic-motivation. The theory was the basis for their 1985 book *Intrinsic Motivation and Self-Determination in Human Behavior*. Springer. Also see the resources from the *American Psychologist* (January 2000) at: https://selfdeterminationtheory. org/SDT/documents/2000_RyanDeci_SDT.pdf

24 See Deci, E. L., & Ryan, R. M. (2012). "Self-Determination Theory." In P. A. M. Van Lange, A. W. Kruglanski, & E. T. Higgins (Eds.), *Handbook of Theories of Social Psychology* (pp. 416–436). Sage Publications Ltd.

25 Freedom in the frame is explored in Cable, Daniel M. (2018) *Alive at Work: The Neuroscience of Helping your People Love What They Do*. Harvard Business Press.

26 Charles Handy is a British social philosopher and writer. See profile at: https://www.london.edu/think/profile-charles-handy-social-philosopher

27 Handy, Charles B. (1978). *Gods of Management: The Changing Work of Organizations*. Souvenir.

28 Excerpt from a summary of the Handy's four cultures: Retrieved from: https://www.mindtools.com/ass7geb/handys-four-types-of-culture

29 See profile: https://www.london.edu/faculty-and-research/contributors/ jules-goddard

30 From Goddard, Jules. (2011) *LBS Business Strategy Review*, Issue 2. See also "Experiments in Management" by Jules Goddard at: https://www.london. edu/think/experiments-in-management

31 Retrieved from SHRM: https://www.shrm.org/resourcesandtools/ hr-topics/talent-acquisition/pages/record-millions-workers-quit-2021-bls-great-resignation.aspx

32 The term "Great Resignation" was coined by Anthony Klotz, a professor and psychologist at Texas A&M. Retrieved from: https://www.bloomberg.com/ news/articles/2021-05-10/quit-your-job-how-to-resign-after-covid-pandemic?

33 PWC Global Workforce. "Hopes and Fears Survey 2022": a survey of 52,195 individuals who are in work or active in the labour market. The full report can be downloaded from: https://www.pwc.com/gx/en/hopes-and-fears/ downloads/global-workforce-hopes-and-fears-survey-2022-v2.pdf

34 PWC Report."Millennials at Work: Reshaping the Workplace." The full report can be downloaded from: https://www.pwc.com/co/es/publicaciones/ assets/millennials-at-work.pdf

35 From a *Leadership Now* article on Fast Company. (29 December 2022) Retrieved from: https://www.fastcompany.com/90825537/leaders-focus-2023

36 Retrieved from: https://group.canarywharf.com/press-release/canary-wharf-group-appoints-a-junior-board-070322/

9

STORYTELLING GLUE

The stories your people share say much about what your organisation does, what is important and how people are regarded.

Professor Sumantra Ghoshal wrote about that early impression you have when you enter a workplace. Memorably, he called it the "smell of the place"[1] – the way you can instantly sense the energy and hum of work and how people walk and talk. As a new employee you can usually sense an even stronger fragrance through the stories people tell. You will quickly learn of heroes and villains, of rising stars and the ones to avoid. Stories of success and failure, of the ideas that were tried and never worked, and lessons never learned. These stories are exchanged and embellished, with details lost or added over time, but they give you a helpful insight into what is unremarkable and yet special about the organisation. Occasionally, you will hear of a maverick leader who does not conform to the norm, and your storyteller will nod sagely at the precariousness of such mischief, whilst

DOI: 10.4324/9781003410690-10

you (now attuned) will sniff a hint of glue. At other times it may be no more than a shaggy dog story.

When I first joined HSBC, I was told the same story by three different people whom I met within the first month. The story was a "true story" of a heroic private banker who had saved a wealthy client from some embarrassment. The client was on Bond Street, a smart high-end road of designer shops in London's West End. He had a big public profile and was out discretely buying his friend an elegant watch. When he tried to pay, his credit card was declined. He did what any self-respecting millionaire would do and rang his bank or, rather, he called his private banker's mobile. The banker, without a moment's hesitation ran from the office across Piccadilly, into the shop, paid for the watch (with his corporate card) and left without any fuss. The client took his friend for brunch in Mayfair, without any of this intervention being remarked upon. The story was shared to illustrate the customer-focused lengths to which the banker had gone to solve his client's problem. The banker had to go to even greater lengths to reconcile the card purchase with the clients' own bank account, but in a market where wealthy clients are multi-banked, these kinds of heroics were the order of the day. I was told this obsession with client service was a hallmark of the place and something that closely connected the bank with its clients. The story, of course, told us many other things about the bank (its clunky fraud procedures, compliance rules, crazy corporate card limits, the possible risks and legalities it raised), but the repeated punchline was: "It just shows the effort we go to never let a client feel let down." Whether the story was true or not did not seem to matter – it was the point of the punchline that made the story sticky.

The stories your people share say much about what your organisation does, what is important and how people are regarded. Such stories can give indications of culture in action: team accomplishments, memorable wins, new product launches, tackling villainous competitors, celebrating heroic successes, as well as sharing the pain of failure. Storytelling can be a smart way of you communicating culture in the way you talk about your business – highlighting examples of collaboration, innovation and experiments, and the outcomes achieved. The hero of the story does not have to be the usual suspect, but may well be an unusual or unsung contributor. The outcome of the tale may not just be a financial goal achieved; it could more likely be a contribution to the wider community, lessons learned and values shared.

For stories about culture, the key narrative device is the use of the pronoun "we". But the typical hero in a business story is almost always the entrepreneurial genius, a Jobs, Ma or Musk and others. But it is the *teams* that they brought together who designed and built the Mac, brought e-commerce to China and sent rockets into space and back again. The leader often takes the limelight, but 48 people were credited inside the Mac, 18 men and women built Alibaba from scratch, and Musk succeeded because he was avaricious in his recruitment of the best talents from other firms. Dolly Singh, the former Head of Talent at SpaceX, describes the brief like this, and it sounds like a scene from science fiction adventure movie:

> I jokingly described myself as the Pied Piper of Super Nerds. My role was essentially to go and find people a thousand times smarter than me and get them excited about solving a really hard problem. One of the ways we explained what the SpaceX culture was, and this was to be really honest with people, was that SpaceX is "Special Forces". We take on the missions that others deem impossible. We told them, this will be the hardest thing you will ever do in your life. We sought the kind of personality that wants to be a [US] Navy SEAL – the engineering equivalent of that.[2]

For several years, storytelling in business seemed to be all the rage. In the 2010s, I attended numerous leadership conferences, seminars and strategy workshops where some enigmatic speaker would have the audience completely captivated as they unpacked the "three beats of the leader's story" or espoused the value of sitting cross-legged around our imaginary campfires to explore the mystery and magic of the storyteller's art. In leadership workshops, jaded executives were encouraged to re-imagine their corporate resume as a "leadership journey" illuminated with moments of personal "epiphany" and hard-won life-lessons. As a welcome relief from the usual death by PowerPoint, storytelling seemed a rich seam to explore. I discovered at one workshop that almost all business and personal challenges could be better understood through some cleverly curated clips from movies. Most memorably, through a deconstruction of *The Shawshank Redemption*,[3] I learned about true friendship, personal resilience, working under pressure and the enduring value of knowing a good accountant.

Some of the conference speakers were as extraordinary in the flesh as they were in the best-selling books they had written: Bear Grylls (broke his back, but then climbed Everest before he was 21); Joe Simpson (survived catastrophic injuries on a mountain, but made life-and-death decisions that haunt him to this day); John McCarthy (held captive in a basement in Beirut for five years, but emerged as man of great warmth and unbelievable tolerance); and Ellen MacArthur (solo-circumnavigated the world in 94 days, but emerged an articulate public champion of sustainability before the topic was de rigour). These days, though, if I attend a business forum, the inclusion of a storyteller on the agenda is now more likely to prompt a world-weary sigh rather than a standing ovation.

The alchemists

Advertisers and marketers once embraced storytelling as the mode through which they would drive up the sales of desirable products. There were some wondrous and very memorable moments, where classic story themes were fused with brand campaigns. Apple's "1984" Mac launch[4] (evoking Orwell's dystopian vision) and the Guinness "Surfer" commercial[5] (narrating Melville's *Moby Dick*) were each brilliantly done: smart, imaginative and thought-provoking.

Two of cinemas' great directors started their careers selling colourful PCs and dark draft beer. Jonathan Glazer, director of "Surfer", went on to make the film *Sexy Beast*, with Ben Kingsley, described by Martin Scorsese as the best British film he had ever seen.[6] Apple's "1984" was the breakout moment for Ridley Scott, who went on to create iconic blockbusters such as *Alien*, *Blade Runner*, *The Martian* and the Academy Award winning *Gladiator*.

The idea of the advertiser as storyteller par excellence may have inspired the writers of the TV series *Mad Men*, where its anti-hero and creative genius Don Draper uses brilliant storytelling to pitch his campaign ideas. In "The Carousel Pitch",[7] Draper's heartfelt epithets and tear-inducing sincerity stuns the executives from new prospective client Kodak-Eastman. His approach is understated, and the tempo at which he delivers the pitch is measured and thoughtful. He features his own wife and young children in close association with the product, making the offer less about the product or the new technology and more about the deep personal connection and emotions the product can create. He tells the client: "It lets us travel the way a child travels. Around and around and back home again. To a place where we know we are loved." Too often we are tempted to bombard our colleagues and customers with detailed data and multiple arguments to prove our point. There are, of course, well-proven diminishing returns in these endless proof-points. The Don Draper character points us towards a simpler, more human-centred way of connecting. When we think about the challenge of change and "taking others with us" there is a delicate, but potent, lesson for us here.

Draper's successful pitch rescues his firm's tenuous place amongst the big agencies on Madison Avenue (New York). But like many of the best stories, there is, of course, a twist. The real magic of the pitch was that, for Don, the performance was nothing more than that – an act. A charade. He had left all authenticity outside in the trash, using his wife and children as mere visual assets to sell his concept. I implore you to watch it and be amazed by the power of the master (and duplicitous) storyteller.

I am less sure the advertisers of today use storytelling with such conviction or skill. Their objective is not the memorable story retold, but the widely distributed meme or gif. The allegorical and metaphorical wit found in adapting Melville or Orwell seem to be seldom bothered with. We are, without much ado, asked to Bet365, or Compare the Meerkat or, more simply, Go Compare.

The advertisers' goal is to gain a momentary mindshare, a nanosecond span of attention, and their creative solution is to treat the audience like kindergarten consumers, grasping for the screenshot-friendly marshmallows on offer. The writer and cartoonist Hugh McLeod summed up the dumbed-down approach beautifully:

If you spoke to people the way advertising now speaks to people, they would punch you in the face.[8]

Death of the story

Technology has played a part in making stories both unbelievably easy to access and, simultaneously, too easy to ignore. Whilst we can readily access more than 30 million books via Amazon, we are a mere thumb-swipe away from the distraction of instantaneous stories of global importance and/or celebrity gossip, super-condensed into a few hundred characters on Twitter. Worse still, the long-form story version of the tweet starts with the soul-destroying tease "Thread". On Instagram, a story is now described as a "slideshow that allows us to capture and post related images and video content, so we share more of our lives with those we are close with". Another thumb swipe and Facebook sends us photo-montage stories of our colleagues' enviable holidays, our half-remembered second-cousin's birthday and our pet's best adventures. Not much room then for Melville's 585 dense pages.[9]

TED Talks have become the modern equivalent of business storytelling. In a puritanically branded event, an over-rehearsed speaker has up to 18 minutes to enlighten, persuade and inform – and hope that their nuggets of knowledge will be worthy enough to be shared by millions online. Depending on your perspective, TED Talks is a medium that has either saved Western thinking and the promulgation of new ideas, or it has not. *Talk Like TED* by Carmine Gallo[10] is a massive business bestseller. And the TED franchise has created a whole industry of training, books, videos and professional tutors to help you "Present Like TED", "Own the Room", and "Rock it Like TED". Airport bookshops are packed with TED's alumni. TED's own editorial has a succinct take on why Storytelling is enormously helpful:

> How do you foster connecting, empathy and understanding between people. Tell a good story, of course.[11]

As you'd expect, in the myriad eclectic topics and more than 3,000 official talks now available, there are duds and some gems. But one of the very best is just five minutes in length, one of the shortest TED Talks ever shared.

"Save the shoes"

The TED Talk story is titled "A life lesson from a volunteer firefighter", by Mark Bezos, sometime more simply "Save the shoes".[12] Like all the best stories, Bezos immediately ignites your imagination. His mode of telling has a theatrical wow factor, walking onto the stage dressed as a fireman, holding his hard hat, and with humility and great humour he shares the story. He seems genuine and authentic, making the story both personal and universal. On a night of much drama when a house is on fire, his only contribution is to rescue the home owners' shoes from the fire. In its punchline and Bezos' brief epilogue, there is a sticky reminder of how powerful lessons can be found in real-life experiences and how great storytelling can still blow up a room. As Bezos finishes, he brings the house down.

> In both my vocation and my avocation as a volunteer firefighter, I am a witness to acts of generosity and kindness on a monumental scale, but I'm also a witness to acts of grace and courage on an individual basis. And you know what I've learned? They all matter. So, as I look around this room at people who either have achieved, or are on their way to achieving, remarkable levels of success, I would offer this reminder: don't wait. Don't wait until you make your first million to make a difference in someboy's life. If you have something to give, give it now. Serve food at a soup kitchen. Clean up a neighbourhood park. Be a mentor. Not every day is going to offer us a chance to save somebody's life, but every day offers us an opportunity to affect one. So, get in the game. Save the shoes.[13]

Time for a reboot?

Bezos's story is about the small acts that get noticed. The leadership shifts needed to create glue are not seismic grand-standing gestures that are showy or political. They are subtler moments – of more time given, of genuine listening and exhibiting different priorities that are recognised and valued by others. Perhaps in Mark Bezos' wonderful tale there are some clues to how storytelling can be made more compelling and fresher for business audiences again. Re-hashing the familiar "heroic endeavour" story now seems outmoded. A more authentic and humbler tale of ordinary achievement and learning can be found more meaningful.

Filmmaker Peter Guber wrote in "The four truths of the storyteller"[14] that being authentic is crucial. For Guber, the story has to be true to the teller, sound true for the audience, ring true in the moment and be true to the mission the storyteller is trying to impart. If it is not, then we see right through it and never suspend our disbelief.

Authentic, smaller stories of collaboration and partnership, of learning, tolerance and listening might trump stories of success hard-won through perseverance, fortitude and single-mindedness. A helpful shift to a greater diversity of storyteller, different cultures, accents and outlooks shared mean we also must listen more attentively to learn. The team effort is often overlooked because it is hard to describe or seems in some way contrived.

But if the story is about "Team Sputnik", or "The New Radicals" or the "Innovators" who came together and did something amazing as part of a change programme, the story can be more memorable and glue-reinforcing than a dull roll-call of names.

A story about Edith Childs

Amid aggressive non-discourse via Twitter, spiky media sound bites and political putdowns, it might seem odd to go to politics to replay a story that might provide us with some clues of where powerful storytelling might find some inspiration. But it is out there if you take time to take a look. Whatever your political persuasion, after taking a peek at Don Draper and Mark Bezos, I urge you to watch a beautifully told story about an unremarkable 60-year-old woman called Edith Childs.

On a freezing night in November 2012, in Des Moines, Iowa, Barack Obama stood before thousands in a town square on the eve of the election.[15] With many hundreds of tales to choose from, after a long brutal campaign, Obama told the story of how Childs, whom he only met once briefly, was the "one voice that changed a room", prompting him to change his outlook, his behaviour and his campaign team's strategy.

It is a story of a leader (Childs, not Obama) galvanising others. She is an unusual character, and Obama describes her as such, but she becomes the motivating force that engages the whole room, re-energising the campaign and inspiring Obama to dig deeper and work harder. If the story he shares does not move you (even a little) then I guess crafting human stories to inspire, energise and ignite others may well have had their day. But I guess, when you see it, you will see what I mean.

At LBS, we sometimes build some form of storytelling element into our Executive Education learning programmes. At its simplest level this might be in the way cohort members are encouraged to introduce themselves to one another (by sharing their story), or at a more sophisticated level, it might be around building a strategic challenge into a compelling narrative that engages and excites others. We use expert facilitators, often writers themselves, as well as actors, stand-up comedians, filmmakers and improvisers to enthuse and build confidence. There are also some very simple ways you might use storytelling in your teams to make better sense of business problems.

Exploring strategic challenges

Business "models" are not always very memorable. We more easily recall *Star Wars*' The Force than Michael Porter's competitive model of Five Forces. When doing team exercises, familiar tales, tropes and characters are good ways to instantly connect ideas and minds.

Why not use a familiar story (movie or book) and get your team to think about a business challenge using a metaphor from that familiar tale? Rather than plot some actions from a hurried SWOT (strength, weaknesses, opportunities and threats), ask the team: "What if you had Harry Potter's magic wand and three spells you could cast? What issues, fixes or gaps would you choose to use them on in your business?" Get them to discern and rank their choices. Alternatively, use a film like the 1980s science-fiction comedy film *Back to the Future* as a launchpad to discuss what your organisation would look like ten years from now and the actions you need to take now for it to survive and thrive in the future.

What do you learn from the stories your people share?

From day one with an organisation, you will hear stories. The water-cooler gossip magnifies stories which get shared year after year. When I joined HSBC in 2005, the grandee Chairman, Sir John Bond, was less remarked upon for his track record of aggressive acquisitions than his rather odd habit of turning out the lights on the upper floors of the building as he left late each evening. When the Bond visited Hong Kong, he was often spotted on the ferry between Central and Kowloon, which costs a fraction of the price of a taxi. Even if the stories were never true, they told a deep underlying truth about HSBC's culture and leadership, which remains, 20 years later, an organisation internally obsessed with the cost of everything.

Social media has become the new default channel for complaints, with users tweeting and retweeting frustration and annoyance when service standards slip, a plane is delayed or a parcel is not delivered. People tend to have less time to post the good news stories that praise the people who fixed the problems. Several years ago (long before Twitter provided a real-time feed), Barclays produced an internal engagement campaign called "Everybody Counts". It farmed hundreds of real stories from employees, customers, suppliers and partners about how and where people in the organisation had done things brilliantly well for the customer.

By exploring and celebrating these stories, it built both engagement as well as a better understanding of the real problems that absorbed staff's time. These real stories were way more compelling than a management consultant's dry analysis or process charts. The bigger challenge was for Barclays leaders: what to do with that powerful insight.

There is something both democratic (we can all tell a good yarn, right?), as well as refreshingly human about exploring a business challenge through the format or metaphor of a story. Stories are familiar, memorable and easily shared. Great stories cross borders and can be translated and adapted for different tastes and cultures. They resonate more than business theory, purpose, vision and the features of a product or service. In the words of the *Mad Men* character Don Draper, using stories creates a "sentimental bond" with your audience, and so a much deeper and more potent connection. Stories are a good way of reinforcing glue.

Applying glue

- Do you have a story about glue? Perhaps a story about the power of teams, or calibration or talent unleashed?
- When new joiners join your firm, what are the stories they hear about the firm?
- What truth, or otherwise, do these shared stories say about the organisation?
- When presenting, can your materials be adapted to illustrate the importance of glue? Can you delegate the telling others? Can you present successes through the experiences of others, with the learning described by them?
- What does the "saving the shoes" moment look like in your firm? What are the small gestures and moments of generosity and help that can be called out and celebrated?
- Is such gratitude often and regularly shared?

Notes and references

1 Ghoshal, S. and Bartlett, C. (1999) *The Individualized Corporation: A Fundamentally New Approach to Management*. Collins Business.

2   The quote is from Episode 2 of the BBC TV documentary series "The Elon Musk Show". (2022) Dolly Singh was the former Head of Talent at SpaceX from 2008 to 2013.

3   *The Shawshank Redemption* is a 1994 American drama film written and directed by Frank Darabont, based on the 1982 Stephen King novella.

4   Apple "1984" Macintosh Computer commercial, directed by Ridley Scott. Retrieved from: https://youtu.be/VtvjbmoDx-I

5   Guinness "Surfer" commercial (with horses). (1998) Directed by Jonathan Glazer. Retrieved from: https://youtu.be/w9ogzVyTtcw

6   Martin Scorsese was speaking at a Q&A at the British Film Institute when he made the remark to the author.

7   "The Carousel Pitch" from the TV series *Mad Men*, Season One, Episode 13. (May 2008) The episode script and quote used here was written by Matthew Weiner and Robin Veith. Retrieved from: https://youtu.be/suRDUFpsHus.

8   Culture Design Group. (31 October 2008) From the brilliant cartoonist and writer Hugh McLeod, who is the founder of a cult company called Gaping Void. See: https://www.gapingvoid.com/blog/2008/10/31/mass-marketing-and-the-heroic-lone-individual/

9   Dore, J. (2019) *Storytelling, Time for a Reboot.* The segment of Twitter text formed part of an article prepared in 2019 for LBS Think, and the quote from Instagram's website was attributed.

10 Gallo, Carmine. (2014) *Talk Like TED: The 9 Public Speaking Secrets of the World's Top Minds.* Macmillan.

11 TED: Ideas Worth Spreading website. Retrieved from: https://www.ted.com/playlists/784/how_to_bring_empathy_and_authenticity_to_your_life

12 "A Life Lesson from a Volunteer Firefighter", by Mark Bezos. Retrieved from: https://www.ted.com/talks/mark_bezos_a_life_lesson_from_a_volunteer_firefighter

13 Transcribed from: https://www.ted.com/talks/mark_bezos_a_life_lesson_from_a_volunteer_firefighter

14 Guber, Peter. (December 2007) "The Four Truths of the Storyteller." *Harvard Business Review.* Retrieved from: https://hbr.org/2007/12/the-four-truths-of-the-storyteller

15 "President Obama Tells the Story of Edith Childs, the Inspiration for 'Fired Up! Read to Go!'" Retrieved from: https://youtu.be/_MjccRjErQw

10

ORGANISATIONAL GLUE

Redesigning and reinventing our organisations requires a more
profound shift.

This book is principally concerned with how to create glue through a
change in leadership approach, but it also points towards a new, more
imaginative, model of the organisation itself. If organisations want to
harness their best people, and better cohere their ambitions with deeper
engagement and closer collaboration, then creating glue will continue to be
key. But to create real transformation, many other dimensions of the firm
also need to change.

The way people are developed, and the way that talent is sought and
retained, needs to be re-adopted as a critical leadership concern. Similarly,
the employee proposition needs to be rethought from one that has become
(in recent years) very much shaped around the individual to one that
is designed to optimise outcomes for the whole firm and its customers.
Firms may need to adjust their performance focus, to be less obsessed

DOI: 10.4324/9781003410690-11

with metrics and measures (what is achieved) and more with meaning (why that matters).

A more profound shift is required

If a deeper transformation is sought, I would propose that firms undertake a more profound shift across four dimensions of the organisation: leadership; people development; their employee proposition; and performance focus (see Figure 10.1).

Leadership style moves from a traditional managerial approach to one more concerned with cultivating others. It becomes less corporate, formal, and supervisory, and more unusual, open and socially engaged. People and talent development moves from managing processes and sponsoring at a distance, to one of deep personal ownership and involvement. It becomes less about big firm-wide initiatives and more about creating talent cohorts that leaders personally know well. The employee proposition moves from a decentralised, individualised contracting model to a more coherent and

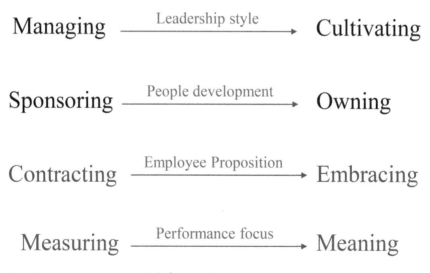

Figure 10.1 An organisational shift is needed

collaborative mode. It becomes less about shaping the proposition around the individual and more about creating a firm that embraces and serves. The performance focus moves from one wholly concerned with the strategic goals and financial results that drive reward to one more concerned with purpose, values and achieving great outcomes for customers. It becomes less about demanding clarity and alignment on traditional performance measures, and more about an intentional and meaningful assessment of success.

I will consider each of these dimensions in turn, before exploring what excellence currently looks like amongst the best modern firms today.

Leadership – from managing to cultivating

Leaders need to shift their concern from managing employees to cultivating people (as illustrated in Figure 10.2).

Consider the typical management style and approach found within most major organisations, capably led by experienced, credible managers, using a common playbook of tools and behaviours. The traditional managing mode is familiar and well understood. The style is often unsurprising: corporate, confident, charismatic and respected, but typically, aloof and guarded. Leaders emphasise the importance of strategic goals and close attention to financial metrics, whilst ensuring clear responsibility, ownership and clarity of objectives. Major change is typically communicated through "set-piece" channels, town halls, e-messaging or via a cascade to line managers and reporting "up the line". These leaders build formal co-operation within the firm through good project management, service level agreements and assurance through supervision and regular status meetings. The best leaders amongst them role-model these playbook rules, honing their personal effectiveness over time. It is the leadership mode that built the great industrial and service enterprises of the last century and early years of this. But is it sufficient for now, in this new age of hybrid working, flexibility and employee ambivalence?

As in Figure 10.2 the shifts from 'Managing' to 'Cultivating' are differences in emphasis (and do not represent an either, or choice) but taken together, they mark out a very distinctive style of leadership. A focus on others does not mean more Managing, it means less. This is not about presenting a right and a wrong way of leading but emphasising a shift

Leadership and management style

Managing	Cultivating
The style of leadership is uniform and corporate. Leaders are confident, charismatic and respected, but personally distant.	The style of leadership is often "unusual". Leaders are readily accessible, socially at ease and more open about themselves.
Leaders build formal co-operation by sponsoring joint projects, internal secondments, agreeing shared KPIs and resources.	Leaders engage widely and deeply, seeking to build social capital, encouraging cross-firm collaboration, networking and strengthening ties.
Leaders prefer "set-piece" communication, town halls, cascade of e-messaging or via line managers, and reporting "up the line".	Leaders prefer informal communication, voice not email, open offices and unplanned engagement, like management by "walking around".
Leaders supervise, with emphasis on regular reporting, functional oversight and formal meetings.	Leaders create an environment of autonomy, emphasising less supervision and providing more latitude to individuals and teams.
Leaders show deep commitment to the firm, its brand and reputation, creating alignment and improved performance.	Leaders share a genuine concern for the organisation's people, creating an environment of psychological safety.

Figure 10.2 Leading with glue requires a shift from the traditional mode

which aims to cultivate people. Leading with glue requires a shift away from the traditional mode of management but it does not mean a complete rejection.

No senior leader is likely to return to the office, absolved of all responsibility for reporting, supervision, risk management or employee performance management. Likewise, no leader can expect to be as successful at motivating others in this new paradigm, without applying more personal time and energy to nurturing the attention and energies of others. As a firm develops more leaders with the same approach, it can gradually move from a traditional organisational model to one that is more widely concerned with cultivating others. This approach fuses the best, most cohesive, behaviours of the past to directly address the deep dissociation many people feel about work.

As we saw in Chapter 5, those who exhibit this new style of leadership are often seen by colleagues and peers as unusual because their approach marks a distinctive shift from the norm. It takes huge amounts of energy for leaders to build relationships across and down through the organisation. In doing so, they show more of themselves, and role-model that as the new leadership norm.

In the meantime, the old traditional approach of close line management, regular reporting and supervision, continues to be presumed or is re-imposed by organisations in a new paradigm of remote, flexible and hybrid working. At least one segment of the workforce is not buying it. In January 2023 at the World Economic Forum (WEF) in Davos, Thierry Delaporte, the chief executive of the IT firm Wipro (which employs 260,000 people worldwide) said:

> 10% of (my) staff don't even check one email per month. They're 25, they don't care. They don't go on their emails, they go on Snapchat, they go on all these social things.[1]

Delaporte argued that employers had to adapt to "destabilising" differences between how corporations and their staff want to communicate. A whole cadre of line managers, supervisors and executives have grown up in a different age from the one now rapidly emerging, and readjustment is difficult. This not about stubbornness on the part of leaders. We have relied on a playbook insufficient for the future of work, and the muscle-memory of that old way of working is hard to lose.

People and talent development – from sponsoring to owning

Leaders need to shift their attention from managing processes and, at arm's length, sponsoring people and talent development, to taking personal ownership of the future of the firm as illustrated in Figure 10.3.

Surprisingly, organisations that pride themselves on careful analysis of product performance, market segmentation and strategy execution still bamboozle their people with an incoherent smorgasbord of people engagement initiatives that come and go like a new spring collection. At times, the way major companies go about investing in their people provokes in me a heady mix of amazement and bemusement. Amazement that so much time, effort and money is still wasted on meaningless broad-brush corporate initiatives; and bemusement that some of the most powerful organisational levers available to the CEO are so often neglected or simply disregarded. As a contrast, you will recall the story in Chapter 2 of Clive Bannister taking personal ownership of global induction and high-potential talent development. Those were powerful levers of glue and he used them to good effect. Clear ownership like this provides valuable focus to development programmes.

HR directors and chief learning officers often ride a cyclical rollercoaster of programme investment which is approved in one year and then abruptly curtailed the next. Areas considered as part of training and development are too easily seen as "discretionary spend", easily cut, deferred or demised. A glue-focused approach means that development money is spent more strategically, in a targeted way, not as broad-brush common training initiatives. Ensuring that ownership of glue-related interventions and development programmes is a senior leadership responsibility, not embedded in the HR department budget, can at least elevate the discussion about investment in this group to the most senior levels of the business. This does not mean glue-related programmes will be immutable in difficult times, but when the decisions *are* made, there might hopefully be some debate.

Ownership also brings greater focus to that spend. For glue, investment is best focused on small talent groups of disaggregated individuals from different parts of the firm. The actual spend involved does not need to be enormous, as the principal cost is the senior management time given to encourage, mentor and promote cohorts and their experiments. Our

People and talent development

Sponsoring	Engaging
Regular investment in broad firm-wide employee engagement initiatives, training, and development courses.	Senior leaders time and resources prioritised towards the identification and development of key groups of talent.
Rigorous performance processes, documented reviews, focus discussions and annual promotions.	Leaders provide regular meaningful feedback, with opportunities for advancement considered and made throughout the year.
High-quality professional management of resourcing and learning, with clear sponsorship of key programmes.	Senior leaders directly engaged in the hiring, induction, development, and retention of the very best people
Project delivery, key performance measures, efficiency and effectiveness is highly valued.	Business experiments are sponsored, highly-valued and celebrated by leaders

Figure 10.3 Leaders are more closely engaged in talent development

galvanising leaders in the early part of this book coveted, handpicked, recruited, poached and embraced the very best talent they could secure to launch their extraordinary ventures. Steve Jobs even disrupted his own organisation, of which he was chairman, by ensuring that the very best talent in Apple was wholly dedicated to his personal Mac taskforce. Sumantra Ghoshal and others have shown that when these talent groups are put together, there is still a particular configuration required (something he calls "combination capability"[2]) for them to be able work optimally. Therefore, my emphasis on you identifying your most valuable people is the best place to start and then you need to build belief and momentum from there.

The crucial talent development shift is one about appropriating ownership. In my experience, interventions are more impactful when senior leaders are directly and personally engaged in the hiring, induction and development of talent, and are strengthened when design, learning partner choices and budgeting are also owned by them, not simply devolved or delegated. (See Figure 10.3 earlier to illustrate this emphasis on ownership.) This may not be popular with HR departments, but they will benefit more from a close partnership with senior leaders rather than pursuing a separate agenda of interventions.

A similar rethink is needed on performance management processes, which are often a bureaucrat's dream, and are too often onerous, unloved and poorly sponsored by senior leaders. A new sense of agility and flexibility for reward is needed, which responds quickly to encourage or keep talent throughout the year – not at some imagined magical inflection point in the calendar – and decisions are more clearly owned by leaders. It may not be the glue-minded leader's most instinctive priority, but many of these legacy processes are irredeemable.

The employee proposition – from contracting to embracing

Leaders need to reconsider the firm's employee proposition, from a decentralised, individualised contracting model to a more coherent and collaborative mode that embraces and includes all (see Figure 10.4).

As we covered in Chapter 8, the aftermath of the Covid-19 pandemic, hybrid working, the "great resignation" and "quiet quitting" have disrupted

Employee proposition

Contracting	Embracing
Decentralised, remote and hybrid working predominates, with little regular office attendance, which remains popular with employees.	An emphasis on the firm's workplace, as a valued resource, a collaboration venue and a source of pride. Flexibility varies, with office attendance encouraged.
Employee benefits and policy are generously shaped around all individuals, with conditions and reward determined by market rates.	Employee benefits, flexible working policy and reward are shaped by the service and collaborative needs of the firm, as they best serve the customer.
"Employees" are variously employed, contracted, temporary or consulting for the firm, with large variances in terms and conditions.	The majority of employees are employed directly by the firm, with broad participation in variable reward or the firm's share scheme.
Control and procedures dominate, with approvals needed for trivial matters and risk aversion common.	An environment of psychological safety, where employees feel able to try new things, experiment and take the initiative.

Figure 10.4 The firm's employee proposition is one that seeks to embrace

the world of work. These workplace trends have been exacerbated by the heightened expectations of "digital natives" (those born in the 21st century) for flexibility, purpose and a commitment to employee wellbeing. Companies have been forced to re-think the proposition of work itself, not just where employees should work, but how to improve the experience of "working" to attract and retain talent.

In recent years, the tech and fintech sectors have become the poster-people for a reimagining of the employee proposition. Videos have gone viral on YouTube and TikTok of Californian tech firms, following beautiful young people in slacks and dress-down designer labels, wandering through bohemian sparsely occupied, exposed-brick offices, then whizzing down internal slides (replacing lifts) to chill out, sipping iced tea with the in-house well-being counsellor, before swinging by a huddle (meeting) to gauge the pulse and share the vibe rating on Slack, then having a nap in the chill-out zone before using the firm's hair salon and booking a three-week break by the coast, as part of the firms' "work from anywhere" policy.

It seems like a parody for some, but it is the de minimis proposition for some sectors, fuelled by extraordinary growth, healthy revenues and a need to attract talented product managers, social-media marketers and user-interface designers. (The highest paid and most sought-after staff – the engineers, software architects and full-stack developers – left the city-centre offices some time ago and connect to these hubs, whilst working, if not actually living, in the cloud.)

I exaggerate to an extent, and it is easy to caricature and parody an exported Silicon Valley culture, that seems cossetted, self-serving and unproductive, but it is the shiny brochure look that many firms now wish to promote. Not only do these new-model firms make work look, sound and appear very different from the late 20th century, work-hard-play-hard "lunch is for wimps" approach modelled on Wall Street, but they have also entered something that looks like an employee-benefits arms race.

Probably the best companies in the world?

Most of us take our steer from the experience of colleagues and friends for recommendations on where the best place to work and develop our careers would be. The proxy route for this insight may also be career and networking sites like Glassdoor or LinkedIn. In April 2022, LinkedIn released its annual Top Companies list[3] identifying the 50 best places in the USA for professionals to grow their careers. Their listing assessed seven pillars: ability to advance; skills growth; company stability; external opportunity; company affinity; gender diversity; and spread of educational backgrounds. There is nothing wrong with the pillars as such, but their methodology and commentary highlight the way firms have become concerned with the same trend: responding to an individual's desire to have work shaped around them.

Amazon ranked No. 1 on the list, followed by Alphabet (Google's parent company) and Wells Fargo, with high places for other large firms such as Apple, IBM, Comcast, Deloitte and Meta. Alphabet offer four "work from anywhere" weeks per year and "no meeting" days; IBM won plaudits for their hybrid working model that allows employees to decide how often they want to be onsite; Comcast "believes that by being yourself, you are empowered to do your best work". Many of the firms did balance their super-flexible remote and hybrid working credentials with improved pay packages, and commitments on training and development; and many stressed the importance of inclusion and diversity, with JPMorgan Chase notable for "tapping into talent pools that have been historically left behind". IBM transformed their onboarding process with "a focus on empathy and engagement" to help remote new hires feel more connected.

At the beginning of 2023, the jobs website Glassdoor published similar research,[4] with tech companies making up 21 of the top 50 firms, and high-paying management consultants like Bain and Boston Consulting Group starring on the list. Again, the accompanying narrative is consistent, noting "flexibility throughout your career", "flexible culture" and firms "committed to diversity, sustainability and employee welfare". As a snapshot of how major hiring organisations are redesigning and describing their proposition (and being recognised for their attractiveness) it highlights the importance of employee-shaped benefits, making flexibility as core to the offer as health insurance is for jobs in the USA. The best new firms ensure this flexibility is key, but also do much more.

Zopa

Take, for example, a relatively small UK-based fintech company called Zopa, which in 2022 ranked No. 3 in Newsweek's "Most loved workplaces in the UK".[5] Zopa was launched in 2005 by a team from the internet banking company Egg. Originally they were the word's first ever peer-to-peer lender, evolving their business model to acquire a full banking licence in 2020. Since then, they have attracted £3 billion in deposits, more than £2 billion of loans on balance sheet, and issued 360,000 credit cards becoming a top 5 credit card issuer in the UK.[6] Even with 850,000 customers they are, by any benchmark, a minor financial services player in the UK market. They have, though, a focus on employee engagement, emphasising flexibility, fairness, equity and inclusion that is more impressive than many of the biggest global banks in the world. Their people proposition is: "Live your best life; maximize your professional skills". Their culture is big on worker input, with half of the performance review based on values co-created by employees, and their benefits package is amongst the most progressive, offering gender-neutral fully paid parental leave of up to 16 weeks for maternity, paternity and adoption.

Zopa's employee engagement score is 74 (the UK average is 45), with a rating of 4.6 out of 5 on Glassdoor. Compare that to Barclays – 4, Santander – 3.8, Lloyds and Natwest – each 3.9. Zopa's minimum salaries are nearly one-fifth higher than the London living wage, and the firm practices workplace flexibility across all its teams, with all employees able to work abroad for up to 120 days per year. They offer enhanced bereavement leave of up to 15 days for all loved ones (and even two days for pet bereavement) and are piloting flexible bank holidays, so "Zopians" can work a religious bank holiday, like Christmas, and exchange it for a different day of year. Whilst the scope of the employee offer is impressive, for Zopa's Chief People Officer, Helen Beurier, it is not the benefits package that makes the firm a distinctive place to work.

> The differentiating factor for us is not our employee benefits, but the way we have built a sense of psychological safety in the firm. The way we, as a leadership team, react and respond to failure is key, ensuring that our people feel they can progress in an environment that is led with clear purpose and values, where trying is supported, and failure is regarded as a normal part of the journey – that's what makes us different.[7]

At modern firms like Zopa the employee proposition is being sharpened like never before, with leaders directly engaged in what that offer should be and how it can be tuned in a way that attracts talent from enormous competitors. They also helpfully stress the type of safe culture they wish to cultivate.

In whichever way these firms position their offer I still feel for the new graduate hire – landing afresh amidst these new "hybrid" firms or having to navigate the meta-verse (or should that be meta-worse?) future version of hybrid working envisaged by some. The best employers have progressed in many ways, but joining a firm where hybrid working is the norm offers a somewhat sad, strange vacuity compared to the experience of a new graduate recruit as recently as the 2010s. The hullabaloo of those early days when new graduates joined these companies has been lost. In the best ever book written about joining an investment bank in the 1980s, Michael Lewis' *Liars Poker* presents us with what now seems an extraordinary first-day scene, as the new graduate trainee suddenly realises that succeeding in this new firm is not just about demonstrating intellect, hard work and wearing well-pressed clothing; it is a tribal, social jungle and work colleagues are already gathered in packs:

> The other trainees appeared to have been in the office for hours. In fact, to get an edge on their colleagues, most had been there for weeks. As

I walked into the training area, they were gathered in packs in the hallways or in the foyer behind the classroom, chattering. It was a family reunion. Everyone knew everyone else.[8]

My scan here of the current marketplace and the positioning of these "best firms to work for" has no particular science to it or definitive conclusion. I do though think the arms race of employee benefits is less important than what is not explicitly expressed by these firms. Whither the sense of collaboration, or how those firms afford autonomy, build a sense of belonging, or fully-employ or stretch competence, so employees can grow and thrive? It is why Helen Beurier's comment about Zopa is so illuminating and distinctive, with "the way we as a leadership team react and respond" being key to the whole employee proposition – making work psychologically safe, innovative, values driven and purposeful.

Redesign and reinvention

If firms were merely wrestling with the triple challenge of changing working preferences, a younger demographics' attitude to work and a need to facilitate productive hybrid working, then their leaders would probably breathe a sigh of relief. There is much else to distract and exhaust those in positions of leadership. Disruptive change is endemic. Change upon change follows more change, at an accelerating rate, and this compounds across societal, political, cultural, intergenerational and technological challenges. If the only permanence is change, then the permanent response needed seems to be one of resilience and reinvention.

Changing organisations and changing leadership cannot be considered independently. Peter Hinssen tours the world researching innovative fast growth companies and advising larger established companies on how to respond to the disruptive forces of what he terms "The Never Normal". Peter is known as an expert on disruptive innovation, and he can explain even the most esoteric cutting-edge technologies with all the glee of an unabashed "geek". But his steer, like Gary Hamel's, is very much about the importance of reinventing leadership and the culture and practices of management as the key to reinventing organisations.

Hinssen talks about the response to disruption having two interdependent dimensions: the organisation needs to be redesigned; and the type of leadership needs to be reinvented. A snippet here from a short film that he produced for Microsoft illuminates both of these challenges:

> The pace of change today is exponential and large organisations are struggling to find and spot new and radical ideas quickly and seem unable to move fast enough to develop their potential. In the 20th century, size was power, but today being big seems to be a disadvantage. Redesign your company in terms of culture, not structure, find leaders who don't want to lead and employees who actually do. Hire thinkers, doers, makers and rule breakers, and trust them, as avoiding risk isn't safe, it stops you from evolving. This is the age of urgency and innovation, fuelled by technology, and you have to be prepared, you have to reinvent yourself.[9]

Redesigning organisations and reinventing leadership will need much thought and imagination in the coming years. Our search for glue is, in part, a source of resilience (though friendships, collaborative networks, support, empathy and listening) and reinvention (new ideas, initiatives, intellectual capital and organisational memory). Much of this book has been about the reinvention of leadership, but this goes hand in hand with Hinssen's requirement for us to "redesign your company in terms of culture".

Many of the great global industrial giants of the 20th century (for example, GE, IBM and Exxon Mobil) have been replaced at the top of the Fortune 500 rankings by technology companies. Many of these firms, such as Apple, Amazon, Alphabet, Microsoft and Meta, began as start-ups, founder led, variously promising us they would "think differently", be "earth's most customer-centric company", "do no harm", "empower every person on the planet to do more" and "bring the world closer together". But as they grew exponentially, their origins in suburban garages, Harvard dormitories or their parents' rented houses, were quickly left behind. Their structures, visible trappings, organisational model (of divisions, functions, departments), business imperatives (customer acquisition, sales, revenues, costs) and their corporate governance is now pretty much the same as any firm from the 20th century and modelled on the great industrial behemoths they replaced.

From the perspective of the boardroom of the elegantly appointed head office, with the same bankers, auditors, lawyers and consultants advising, the changing of the old order now looks a lot like the past. But if Hinssen is right, and we are entering a new "never normal" age of accelerating change, even more disruptive than the past years of the 21st century, what might the future shape of firms be like? What will be the dominant performance culture that shapes those firms? And how will people know they are succeeding?

Performance focus – from measuring to meaning

The performance focus moves from one concerned with the strategic goals and financial measures that determine reward, to one more concerned with creating meaning for customers and employees.

It seems unlikely that value creation, financial performance and clarity about strategic goals will become any less important in the boardroom, but there also seems to be a next generational employee demand for a more purposeful and meaningful set of goals and measures. Gallop report[10] that, across all ages, there is a demand for ethical leadership and, amongst younger employees, a desire for the firm to be more ambitious on environmental, social and governance (ESG) criteria. My shorthand for this is that younger employees want to be challenged to perform against meaningful goals, not just hit the numbers. These goals can be documented at length and many firms already invest much in comprehensive ESG measures, sustainability reporting and wordy values statements. My suggestion is that employees sense more meaning in working closely with ethical leaders who role-model behaviours, showing consistent and genuine ownership of those goals. The language used by these leaders reflects those values. The organisation itself is described, labelled and signposted with that clear purpose in mind. We are back in Hangzhou at Alibaba in 2010, amongst 14,000 young women and men cohered around an ambition to create the best internet company in the world and serve 100 million aspirant entrepreneurs throughout China.

Perhaps the concerns of this new generation of workers, consumers and stakeholders will become paramount? Will we see the growth of close, human-centered, purpose-driven firms, with their resilience and growth founded on leaders and employees cohered around shared values? (See Figure 10.5 earlier.) Some see other trends of new technology and AI as just too compelling for this model to survive. Will we instead see the emergence of Decentralized Autonomous Organisations (DAOs) – co-operative firms operated by rules encoded as computer programs anchored to the blockchain? These decentralised firms are an amalgam of resources, technology, knowledge and people, transacting and creating

Performance focus

Measuring	Meaning
The importance of strategic goals, leaderships' ownership of these and clarity of the businesses objectives is understood.	Organisational purpose and values are straightforwardly described and clearly understood, with customer centricity a key concern of all.
The firm is structured in terms of distinct departments, with clear reporting lines, management responsibility and spans of control.	The firm is organised described in terms of broad groupings, with co-located teams, arranged to serve customers or as shared functional groups.
Innovation, acceleration units and new acquisitions are managed as separate, standalone business units.	Innovation, acceleration units and new acquisitions are developed as part of the main business and in shared visible locations.
Financial results, business performance metrics and targets predominate, with outcomes determining reward.	Leaders emphasise the importance of purpose, values and customer centricity, recognising personal contributions.

Figure 10.5 The firm's strategy and purpose is more intentional

value with almost instant flexibility, agility and adaptability. There seems little heart or soul in that model, but the huge investment in crypto-currency and AI suggests that we will see speculative capital seek out that intangible model of the firm, not the former. The human dimension will be even more diminished.

Thankfully, the evolution of the firm is a marathon, not a sprint. Whilst the lure of the decentralised model is intriguing, the coming decade will see many new start-ups, family-owned businesses, entrepreneurial ventures, and organisational experiments within larger firms, which seek to redesign the firm, and reinvent leadership in a more human and customer-centric way. I am hopeful that whatever design these organisations take, their people and their culture will be imbued with glue.

Searching for Xanadu

But what if every employee, manager and new starter, was already part of an organisation imbued with glue? What if every single person in the organisation was creating glue? What if the CEO and their senior team understood that from day one, and glue was central to the way the firm was led and managed? What if all new joiners were inculcated into an environment of glue from day one? What if they led an organisation where autonomy, belonging and competence were at the heart of the way the place worked, and that employees regularly scored their own firm as one of the best places to work, and so they wanted to stick around for years? This would be a firm to which talent would flock and feel stretched, and customers would be delighted and recommend their friends. Could such a glue-filled Xanadu[11] firm exist?

Professor Gary Hamel is one of the leading strategy, management and enterprise leadership writers, teachers, thinkers and consultants on the planet.[12] He has spent much time since the 1980s researching, consulting and guiding strategy, advising the c-suite executive leaders of some of the best organisations in the world. In particular, he has examined those firms that have sought to re-engineer the typical management model and unburden their employees from the "bureaucratic bullshit" (his term) that dominates too much of corporate life. If we went looking for the very best firms, which were more human, with leaders finding ways to better engage and unleash talent, Gary Hamel should know where to look.

Humanocracy

I first had the pleasure of meeting Gary Hamel in 2004 at a Human Resources conference in Harrogate, UK. When I say "met", I was in fact sat some distance away in the plenary audience, with about 3,000 other delegates, so "met" is probably stretching the point. It was, though, one of those keynotes that made the hair on your neck stand up. He was passionate, incisive, armed with real-world data and, even from a distance, seemed angry with me personally for working for an organisation that had failed so miserably to inspire and engage the vast majority its people. Hamel memorably challenged the delegates' complacency:

> Most organisations are not getting the passion, creativity and initiative out of their people. They get intelligence, diligence and obedience, but you can get that from a cocker spaniel.[13]

Some years later, I have had the pleasure to meet and work with Gary Hamel at London Business School, and his verve, conviction and way with words remains undiluted.

In 2020 Hamel published a book called *Humanocracy: Creating Organisations as Amazing as the People Inside Them*.[14] Co-written with Michele Zanini, it is a manifesto for a radically different kind of organisation, management style and approach – one so far beyond the common experience of many employees it could risk reading like a fantasy utopian piece. Hamel and Zanini make the case for why organisations need to change: the sapping burden of bureaucracy, the untapped innovation and creativity, and the patently moral case for making work more engaging, not dispiriting and de-humanising. They then produce numerous case studies to substantiate an alternative type of firm, and one that becomes not only believable but compelling.

Their book profiles firms like Morning Star, Nucor and Southwest Airlines in the USA, Vinci and Michelin in France, Handelsbanken in Sweden and Buurtzorg in the Netherlands. These companies are the exceptions that prove the rule, a new vanguard of organisations (and leaders) that have adopted a series of protocols and an approach to engaging and enabling talent that is profoundly different. The essence of this difference takes some detailed exploration, and Hamel and Zanini codify the common attributes and describe a series of guiding principles.

I cannot do justice to their research here, but in the fascinating case studies, there are some common themes for this new more "human-centred" type of organisation. Providing greater autonomy is key, with employees given more independence for decision-making and freedom to implement new ideas. At Burtzoorg, a Dutch healthcare provider, there are almost no managers in an organisation of several thousand, and very few employed in the traditional head-office control functions. At Handelsbanken, a European commercial bank, almost all lending decisions are made autonomously (of head office) by managers in the countries and regions who, crucially, are trusted as they know their customers intimately.

In some of the firms featured, reward has been re-thought, with the upside of good performance being more equitably shared and (for example, at Nucor) bonuses are paid on a team basis, not to individuals. The authors describe organisations in less corporate terms: as "communities", "teammates" or, as Nucor's John Ferriola describes his firm as "more of a family than a company".[15] Hamel goes further than this, talking about organisations and the people within them not as staff, workers or employees (and never as "human capital, as if they were some inanimate asset) but as human beings, with feelings and emotions, and real lives lived vividly, in and outside of work.

He sees firms like Morning Star and Nucor not just as businesses, but as fulfilling a deep human need: "We need more than mere co-workers; we need advocates, allies, and mates – workplace friends who are sympathetic and stalwart."[16] This value found in the workplace took me back into the realm of Robert Putnam's plea for revival in *Bowling Alone* for "more family-oriented workplaces, which allow for the formation of social capital on the job".[17]

Hamel applies this familial, empathetic mode to senior leaders too, who should be unashamed to be open and humane:

> In interpersonal encounters, look for opportunities to reveal something of yourself, and encourage others to do the same. Have a tender heart for those who are struggling with issues outside of work . . . Hire for compassion, follow the golden rule, and celebrate acts of kindness.[18]

In the case studies in *Humanocracy*, and in particular in firms like Nucor and Southwest Airlines, Hamel and Zanini provide a compelling glimpse into workplace cultures that appear rare and unusual. They also make the case for these firms outperforming peers, not just on engagement metrics or retention, but outperforming the market for growth, value creation and profitability. These are not, though, firms who have achieved this by making some sudden pivot to a radical new management model; each has been carefully building their own type of organisational glue over many decades.

Meanwhile in the UK, in plain sight, on the high street and on the worldwide web, there has been since the 1970s, an unusual organisation, imbued with its own particular flavour of glue, from which much can be learned.

The Richer Sounds story

Julian Richer started buying and selling hi-fi separates at school when he was 14. He co-founded Richer Sounds[19] in 1978, and led and managed the business for 41 years until he divested ownership of the business in 2019, which he did in a remarkable way. Richer is, in many ways, an unusual leader, with a view of business and a perspective on life and work that is informed by his deep conviction about ethical practice and, in later life, shaped by his Christian faith. He was just 19 years old when he opened his first shop near London Bridge, selling hi-fi, TV and audiovisual kit. The store was a hit and became listed for over 20 years in Guinness World Records as achieving the highest sales per square foot of any retail outlet in the world.

The business grew across the UK and today it now trades from 52 stores across the UK as well as online and through a telesales and business to businesss operation. Many of the shops' employees have side-hustles as DJs, are musicians and music producers, and through Richer Unsigned, a not-for-profit unit, the firm provides a free platform for over 3,000 unsigned bands and artists. By 2019, Richer had built what he calls a "responsible business" to a turnover to more than £200 million a year. The whole business shared in the value created, with reward fairly distributed amongst employees, and also with 15% of the company's profits donated to some 400 charitable causes. His belief on treating staff well is not just a moral choice, it's a business imperative:

> There is, of course, a cost involved: paying your people above the minimum and going the extra mile for customers, and even paying your suppliers on time. But the financial payback is huge. I am talking about savings from recruitment and training because your labour turnover will be tiny. Your best people who have the most experience will stay – they are a valuable commodity you surely want to hang on to. Your staff will take less time off for sickness and your shrinkage will be minuscule.[20]

A Richer legacy

Richer was interviewed in 2013, and announced, with some wit, that he had made plans to hand his entire business to his employees when he dies, saying he lacked a "spoilt child to run the business".[21] Three years later, then aged 60, he announced that he had transferred ownership to his employees by passing 60% of his shares to a trust. Each of his 500 employees, excluding directors, received a thank-you bonus of £1,000 for every year of work, with eight years' service being the average tenure.

He continues to be a vocal proponent of ethical business, writing a column in The Sunday Times, publishing a book in 2018 called The Ethical Capitalist,[22] and regularly speaking about business ethics, employee engagement, fairness and transparency. His legacy remains a firm that still makes much of its unusual ownership structure and distinctive culture, recruiting based on natural friendliness, rather than high-pressure sales skills. The ethical approach was a founder passion, but it is also one that secured commitment and loyalty from staff and remains ingrained in the business today.

The "responsible business" is an unusual model, but by retaining an employee-owned structure, clear convictions and explicit values, backed by generous giving, it creates a particular kind of glue between employer and employee, which in turn wins loyalty and recommendation from customers, securing numerous Which? Best Retailer awards.

Richer believes that leaders should put business in the service of society, and provide a new kinder, fairer form of capitalism. In his book he argues that ethically run businesses don't prioritise the bottom line, as others do; rather, they are more motivated, innovative and efficient through their ethical practices. There are many areas on which a business should choose to focus; growth, profitability, sustainability, but for Richer it is more fundamentally a choice about doing the right thing, and at the heart of that is the leader's role in treating employees well.

Our philosophy is that staff should come first.[23]

Applying glue

- Read Gary Hamel and Michele Zanini's Humanocracy (see Notes and references for details). It is phenomenally good and relevant if you are interested in management innovation. They also share many terrific free video and learning resources on their website: https://www.humanocracy.com
- Be careful of the language your firm uses; people are not "assets", "human capital" or "resources" to be deployed. They are people with names, lives, families, hopes, dreams and souls.
- What are you already doing to "reinvent" your leadership style?
- How ready would your firm be to make an even more imaginative shift?
- Julian Richer created a particular kind of glue, which aligned wholly with his values as a person. What might that look like where you work?

Notes and references

1 The Daily Telegraph. (17 January 2023) "Bosses Forced to Contact Staff on Instagram as Gen Z Ditch Email." Thierry Delaporte, chief executive of Wipro, which employs 4,500 people in the UK and 260,000 globally, said around 10% of his staff "don't even check one email per month."

2 Ghoshal, S. and Nahapiet, J. (April 1998) "Social Capital, Intellectual Capital, and the Organizational Advantage." *The Academy of Management Review*, Vol. 23, No. 2 pp. 242–266 (25 pages). See also Chapter 3 of this book, "The Advantage of Glue".

3 LinkedIn reports: https://www.linkedin.com/pulse/top-companies-2022-50-best-workplaces-grow-your-career-us-/

4 Glassdoor report: https://www.glassdoor.co.uk/Award/Best-Places-to-Work-UK-LST_KQ0,22.htm

5 Newsweek. "The UK's 100 Most Loved Workplaces." Retrieved from: https://www.newsweek.com/rankings/most-loved-workplaces-uk

6 Source: https://www.zopa.com/investor-information

7 From an interview with the author. (January 2023)

8 Lewis, M. (1989) *Liar's Poker*. WW Norton & Co.

9 Peter Hinssen speaking on a Microsoft sponsored trailer. Retrieved from: https://www.youtube.com/watch?v=Hgh_2k5jFJo

10 Gallop. (30 March 2021) "4 Things Gen Z Millennials Expect from their Workplace." Retrieved from: https://www.gallup.com/workplace/336275/things-gen-millennials-expect-workplace.aspx

11 Xanadu is a mythical place mentioned in Samuel Taylor Coleridge's poem as the place where Kublai Khan built a giant dome. That name came to be associated with magnificent splendour and leisure.

12 Gary Hamel is one of the world's most influential and iconoclastic business thinkers. He has worked with leading companies across the globe and is a dynamic and sought-after management speaker. Hamel has been on the faculty of the London Business School for more than 30 years and is the director of the Management Lab. See also: www.garyhamel.com

13 Quote from the stage of the 2004 CIPD Conference in Harrogate, UK. See: https://www.personneltoday.com/hr/cipd-conference-quotes-harrogate-2004/

14 Hamel, G. and Zanini, M. (2020) *Humanocracy: Creating Organisations as Amazing as the People Inside Them*. Harvard Business Review Press. See also: Humanocracy.com

15 Ibid., p. 78.

16 Ibid., p. 174.

17 Putnam, R. (2000) *Bowling Alone*. Simon Schuster.

18 Hamel and Zanini, op. cit., p. 174.

19 Richer Sounds, which has 52 stores, refuses to use zero-hours contracts and is one of the few companies in the UK with a pay gap that favours women. Employee perks include access to company holiday homes around the world, including in European cities such as Paris, Venice and Barcelona. The company donates 15% of profits, with employees deciding where that money is sent. The company is also a part of the Living Wage Scheme, set up by the Living Wage Foundation, and founder, Julian Richer, has backed their Living Hours programme, which seeks to curb zero hour contracts. Source: Richer Sounds website (see note 20) and company profile.

20 Source: https://www.richersounds.com/sound-advice

21 The Independent. (19 November 2013) "'I Lack a Spoilt Child to Run the Business': Hi-fi Tycoon Julian Richer to Leave Company to His Staff." Retrieved from: https://www.independent.co.uk/news/uk/home-news/i-lack-a-spoilt-child-to-run-the-business-hifi-tycoon-julian-richer-to-leave-company-to-his-staff-8950240.html

22 Richer, J. (2018) *The Ethical Capitalist: How to Make Business Work Better for Society*. Random House Publishing.

23 Retrieved from: https://www.richersounds.com/sound-advice: "I talk about the five elements of staff motivation: fun/happiness, recognition, communication, rewards, and loyalty. The last of these, in my opinion, is the most important because it underlines the sincerity of all your other actions. Our definition of the loyalty we aim to provide might best be described as "a care above and beyond what would normally be expected by an employee."

11

APPLYING GLUE

A way forward for creating personal glue.

This book proposed at the outset that leadership is not about you but about the need to refocus your efforts on others, harnessing talent, configuring diverse teams and building greater cohesion in your organisation. But, if you have got this far, I hope that you feel that the exploration of this book has also served as a suitable investment in yourself. You can, of course, go further. The learning, which is formulated on rigorous evidence-based studies, mirrors the numerous real-life observations made about of leaders and their organisations. The academic evidence and research described in this book can be explored in more depth, and various suggestions for further reading are shared later in the Resources section if you wish to dig a little deeper.

Hopefully, the stories shared help to highlight the pivotal role "glue-minded" leaders play in more effectively engaging across the firm and getting the most out of their people. I am sure you will have your own experiences and learning, through working with inspiring colleagues and

DOI: 10.4324/9781003410690-12

experiencing those "aha moments" that build a sense of belief that we all need in work and life. Whilst the focus throughout this book has stressed the importance of others – building valuable social-capital – ultimately, the responsibility for doing that often circles back, looks for an owner, and that may well mean you.

As we have seen, there are two important dimensions to the way glue is created and nurtured: through your personal actions and visible behaviours; and the environment you create for your people. But I can offer the same proposition with only a small edit and the glue is actually much more likely to materialise. Glue is created and nurtured through the personal actions and visible behaviours of all of your firm's leaders, and the environment they create for their people.

Glue creation, by definition, is not a solo venture. The leaders I have worked with who made the most glue across the firm kept great people very close to them. These adjacent colleagues were invaluable, balancing some of the leader's weaknesses with their own unique contributions, sometimes literally "holding the fort" whilst their glue-minded leader went (metaphorically) into the wilds, building allies amidst the forest and fields in the furthest reaches of the firm. Perhaps you can proactively work with someone else, who supports you in your mission to visibly cultivate glue, but in your own particular way? Or maybe you are that invaluable ally, making sure that, in the execution of a more collaborative approach, outcomes are captured and measured?

With that opportunity in mind, here are some of the key concepts that I hope you have found useful and some ideas that you might reflect on:

- Creating and nurturing glue is your **most important leadership task**. Given the worsening trends of engagement and dissociation, it has never been more important than now. You may already feel that you are deeply immersed in the challenge of deepening engagement amongst your best people, but how might you free up even more time to invest in creating glue?
- You know the critical importance of building **social capital** through cultivating beneficial relationships, collaborative networks and connecting talented cohorts to form an organisational advantage for your firm. Social capital is a key ingredient of glue that you can personally nurture, strengthening the bonds between one another, the organisation and your customers.

- You can **galvanise** talented employees through mandating strategically important innovation-led experiments or enabling groups to work together on things that excite and energise them. Someone once said "the hotter the furnace, the harder the steel". The challenges ahead do not have to be framed as such, but tough challenges met together can forge real personal bonds, and not just metaphorically.
- You need to practise unusual "super-power" leadership behaviours like **listening**, and actively **engaging** widely and deeply across the firm. After an exhausting week, it takes a significant investment of time and energy to walk the floors, stay for the leaving-card presentation, or go out of your way to give time, advice, mentoring or other good gestures, but in doing so, you will show more of yourself and role-model that as the leadership norm.
- The glue-creating firm is one where your employees are given more **autonomy**, deepening their sense of **belonging**, whilst their **competencies** are fully employed and valued. You could grant more autonomy tomorrow and it would be noticed like you would not believe.
- Your senior colleagues can get a sense of glue in action by rethinking the way they work together on developing future strategy. The value found in adopting **clear principles** of workshop design, and the importance of bringing in perspectives from the outside, the customer's voice, or input from "next-generation" employees, cannot be overstated.
- Being more open, engaged and sharing more of **yourself**, will probably mark you out as a little unusual, but this is unequivocally, a good thing.

These are just a few ideas, born out of the many essential ingredients needed to create and maintain glue. The approach you take, in whatever small way, is aimed at creating organisational glue. All other capabilities being equal between your firm and your competitors, it could be the glue you create that differentiates your offer. It could be the thing that makes your best people stay and revitalises your own contribution and impact.

Build social capital

The importance of investing in social capital is not just worthwhile for better collaboration; it can, if configured thoughtfully, be used for what

Ghoshal described as "organisational advantage". I have come back to this well-worn point (perhaps overstated, you may feel) because it is key to the whole proposition. Connecting groups of smart, normally disaggregated people, into cohorts, can create new intellectual capital, and potentially, from this will flow new ideas, initiatives and value can be created. You need to find ways for disparate and diverse talented employees to be able to readily access one another. This is seldom going to work as an invitation to an old-fashioned "training course" or hastily cobbled together "task force" to work on a neglected business project. It needs real imagination to gather not just attendees, but fully engaged participants, and it needs to be designed professionally and purposefully.

For teams who would normally work remotely from one another, there is more complexity to the arrangements – but the principle stands: find ways to design and produce engaging, energising reasons for meeting, talking, socialising and being human again. If possible, remove the artifice and compromise of hybrid participation and make it wholly online or, immeasurably better, wholly in person. All programme evaluations I have seen from before, during and post-pandemic restrictions at LBS have proven the value of face-to-face interaction for learning, engagement and action planning. The worse scores have been for hybrid experiences. We opened Chapter 1 with the true story of the impersonal AI generated interview screen as the preferred hiring filter for a top university. Hybrid solutions for the purpose we have described here add little beyond that cold anonymity for participants staring out or peering into the room. The explosion in online learning serves a purpose and a market need, and broadens access to millions, but I have seen no evidence it creates any glue. If the object is openness, warmth and friendship, bring people together.

If you do bring people together, it is important that the participants expect that this will be time well spent (not just meeting and mingling for its own sake), so that they will be motivated to connect, follow up and stay connected. If you find ways to get this configuration of circumstance (an event or series of events) and motives right (its strategically important, with senior sponsorship), it can also serve to improve relationships, build higher levels of trust and strong bonds amongst the group. If you put something important, meaningful and purposeful at the heart of the agenda, then the contributions are likely to be more personally felt and the outcomes more collectively sought.

The HPDP China cohort mentioned in Chapter 2 was the best example I have seen of this, but few organisations have the scale, budget, resources or inclination to connect large cohorts in exotic locations like that. Recently, I worked with a UK-based property surveyor who brought 30 young managers together for one day with their CEO in East London. For the venue they hired a meeting "room" in the loft space above a salmon-smoking factory. A number of factors were smart in the design. The company founder telling great stories, the proximity to the Olympic Park, the clarity and openness of the CEO, and the creativity of the learning manager who had designed the day combined to great effect. The property team event did not have the enormous investment costs of a trip to China, but in the apparent energy created amongst the managers, and their obvious commitment to find ways to keep connected and make more of their newly extended network was, in many ways, just as impressive. The venue smelt a little odd, but as a glue creation event, it was tremendous.

You may not have done a rigorous talent search yet, and challenged the scope of that search for breadth, depth and diversity, but you will have some sense already of what talent looks like in your organisation. So, why not start small? Perhaps a local or regional event, connecting those from different units and offices, from different backgrounds, with a different perceptive to you, and each with a valuable view on the future. Try some of the ideas shared here and see who else wants to join in? After experience and reflection, some things just might not land, but the approaches that do work can be extended, using glue as part of future changes you are required to lead within your organisation. You may well find it hard to win unplanned funds from the HR department, and your firm's policy may still be negative about face-to-face events. In my experience, the best route, given those obstacles, is to build something around a planned customer event, where marketing or sales budgets have already been secured. The other route is to follow the best leadership advice I was ever given; it is better to ask for forgiveness than to seek permission.

Super-power behaviours

The leadership behaviours of the various glue-minded leaders mentioned in this book are highly sophisticated and too complex to properly document or do any justice to here. Their context, challenges and approach each varied enormously, so my generalisations are offered with that huge caveat. But some general exhibited traits, that were regularly observed to make a difference, were their ability to galvanise, listen and engage broadly and deeply in their firms. This made a difference and their day-to-day approach (making time for others, being actively visible in the workplace, being open and accessible, connected widely, learning and remembering names) made them seem, at times, a little unusual amidst the hustle and bustle of busy, time-poor senior colleagues. They were also able to find imaginative ways to galvanise disparate groups of people.

Consider what would be the topic, challenge or idea around which you might try to galvanise a group of talented people? If unsure, gather them together anyway and see what they are passionate about. With one firm I worked with, the focal point that emerged was not the firm, or business strategy itself, but a charitable cause around which a group cohered following the death of a much loved and well-regarded colleague: getting together afterwards, training, fund-raising and riding together from London to Paris. There were met at the Arc de Triomphe by the CEO (who himself had some health problems) and the firm "pound-for-pound" matched all funds that had been raised.

Autonomy, Belonging, Competence

In Chapter 8 we looked at research about Self-Determination Theory (SDT), which has created much interest and intrigue, since most psychological and management theories of motivation stress extrinsic factors like reward and incentives. But SDT emphasises the importance of fundamental psychological needs. To satisfy these innate needs, leaders need to work hard to give their people more autonomy, encourage a deeper sense of belonging, through strong relationships, and to enable employees to fully apply and develop their talents, or "competencies". The hard work referred to here is bread and butter to the glue-minded leader. This gift of autonomy – of implicit and explicit trust – sometimes seems impossible in firms where control functions, compliance and risk dominate management thinking and procedures, but the best leaders operate like air-traffic controllers, allowing the pilots room to manoeuvre and, once in open-skies, wide parameters to navigate.

Experimentation

Hopefully you are already using experiments or are at least intrigued by the idea. Jeff Bezos famously flagged experimentation as core to Amazon's culture and success, explaining in one of his shareholder letters:

> Failure and invention are inseparable twins. To invent you have to experiment, and if you know in advance that it's going to work, it's not an experiment.[1]

Even at Amazon, things started small and built slowly over time. It took over a decade for Amazon to inculcate experimentation, adopting the "fail-fast-learn" approach, which reportedly now results in over 12,000 experiments each year, each designed to continuously improve customer experience.[2] As we saw, Husqvarna Group used one well-designed experiment to help support the investment case for a brand-new product line. You will not strike gold with anything like that hit rate, but the form, format and thinking created in experiment groups is a different kind of corporate gold, collaborative glue.

Organisational glue

Many mature organisations still spend much thought, time and money wrestling with defining their organisational purpose. Some new start-ups begin with that conundrum before even shipping a single product, holding to Sinek's memorable refrain: "People don't buy what you do; they buy why you do it."[3] Julian Richer did not delay opening his first shop until he had defined precisely what he meant by a truly "Responsible Business". He started by selling consumer electronics, and then spent 40 years building, cultivating and reinforcing the right way to do that, ensuring his staff were well treated and that their achievements were celebrated along the way. But because of that distinctive culture, and a deep-shared sense of doing things differently, employees stuck around for many years, and those remaining when he retired received more than just a cash bonus as the founder's legacy. He passed over to them the firm. It is quite a story built around an inspiring leader, but is also one delivered seven days a week, in 52 high-street shops, and on the web, by the concerted effort of over 500 committed people, somehow imbued with a kind of common glue.

The exact formula for creating glue will vary in every firm. Depending on your own perspective, Richer Sounds may look a small quirky organisation or an enormous complex venture. Whatever the size of your organisation, the vital relational dimensions of "one another", the "organisation" and for "customers" are the ones you are seeking to strengthen. Some firms increasingly think about "customers" in a broader sense to encompass other stakeholders including the communities where they serve and the environment they impact. My argument for investment in glue is that the enterprise grows and thrives because of the strong bonds between these three elements, and this applies if you are part of small start-up enterprise or a large global business.

The key is to start small, experiment, reflect, learn and build, but the most important step, is to start.

A matter of life and death

Much is now being made of a new future for digital, a "metaverse" where we can live our lives vicariously in some three-dimensional world, meeting cool people, trying new things, experimenting with self, going to unfamiliar places and finding someone to love. For some it is a new nirvana – a beautiful future, where anything is possible. But surely our employing organisations, our best firms, our workplaces and new enterprises in the real world should still be able to fulfil much of that promise today? It seems the trends show that many people are not seeing their workplaces in such terms, and many prefer to stay at home to plug and play.

The psychologist Susan Pinker gave a talk in 2017 about the Italian island of Sardinia, which has six times as many centenarians as the mainland, and ten times as many as North America. She became intrigued about why some people live longer and, deploying findings from a detailed research study,[‡] she presented all the likely factors and predictors of longevity. She listed many, including the obvious candidates like clean air, hypertension, weight, whether you drink, whether you smoke, or how much exercise you take. But surprisingly, two of the most important factors were an emphasis on close personal relationships and face-to-face interactions.

The top predictors are two features of your social life. First, your close relationships. These are the people that you can call on . . . that little clutch of people is a strong predictor, if you have them, of how long you'll live. And then something that surprised me, something that's called social integration. This means how much you interact with people as you move through your day. How many people do you talk to? And these mean both your weak and your strong bonds, so not just the people you're really close to, who mean a lot to you, but, like, do you talk to the guy who every day makes you your coffee? Do you talk to the postman? Do you talk to the woman who walks by your house every day with her dog? Do you play bridge or poker, have a book club? Those interactions are one of the strongest predictors of how long you'll live.[5]

So, as we began, we find a reminder again of Robert Putnam's Bowling Alone, though the stakes are not just about community bonds, but about the likelihood, or otherwise, of a longer life. As we saw in Chapter 3, Putnam feared for the loosening and broken social bonds in communities and towns, symbolised in the demise of after-work bowling clubs. But what does this quirky story about Sardinia's centennials have to do with the world of work? In a corporate world that is becoming more remote, our organisations can – even now – still provide a form of social nourishment which, if Susan Pinker is right, is not just life-affirming, but could be life-extending.

It will not feel that way during the hassle of the crowded commute, but maybe buying that coffee and catching-up with a colleague in-person over lunch might be the best form of interpersonal workout either of you will enjoy that day? For some, struggling, mainly at home and "scrolling alone", that brief moment of shared-humanity – which seems so trivial and is easily taken for granted – might not be something that extends a life, but it might be something that makes a working day tolerable, again.

How do you make it stick?

Glue is vitally important, even if it does not seem to be. Not everyone will instinctively buy this idea called glue. The ideas mentioned and the stories shared in this book are fairly broad but represent only a tiny glimpse into the world of glue-minded leadership. I am certain there are thousands of untold stories and experiences of leaders trying to create an organisational advantage, by breaking down barriers, better connecting and cohering talent. In time, there might be a best-practice approach to glue and even academic research on what works well. For now, any good practice, any small experiment, any moment of humanity, seems vital and urgent.

If nothing else, I hope this book provokes more glue stories and ideas to be shared and more discussion amongst business leaders about what can be done to respond to a tide of individualisation, generational-disconnect and employee disengagement. For practical application context is everything, and the concepts here will need to be adapted for your organisation, your market, as well as the work mode and the mood of your firm. All that said, I am mindful that organisations – indeed, perhaps you personally – have already tried a whole range of ideas and initiatives to respond to this trend of employee disengagement.

Making working more palatable

You might not be in the vanguard of the employee-benefits "arms race" that has gripped some sectors, but most readers here will work for firms where employees will have benefited in recent years from improvements in the way that their work is organised, managed, and the technology platforms that they are able to access in the office or remotely. Many of your employees can now work flexibly, or remotely, earn a fairer reward, with gender gaps increasingly scrutinised, and more proactive attention paid to other measures of inclusion, equity and diversity. Firms are becoming less corporate in other ways. Many staff are allowed to wear ripped jeans and slogan t-shirts even when they come in the office. Previously conservative airlines are loosening rules on dress, tattoos and piercings. Some employees can attend an online mindfulness class at lunchtime and watch a beautifully produced seminar on the firm's future strategy, live from anywhere in the world. Some more enlightened firms let office staff munch free gourmet sandwiches and fresh fruit whilst scanning the corporate intranet, pre-loaded with online development tools and learning resources from the best business schools and learning institutes. Some firms have in-house Friday bars, hairdressers, private healthcare and running tracks on the roof. But the Gallop survey will tell us that employee engagement levels are at an all-time low, and the trend is worsening, not improving. A new upward trend of "quiet quitting" made the news globally in 2022, but it seems that despite all your HR department's best endeavours, many employees have been mentally and emotionally checking out from work for much longer.

Ultimately, much of the thoughtfulness and benefits enhancement aimed at making "working" more palatable will be pointless if the work itself is not made more fulfilling. Too many smart professionals are wearied by the humdrum of the bureaucratic tasks, delegated by absentee managers, with hours spent analysing and re-presenting budget numbers for HQ, before heading with a renewed sense of purpose to a place called anywhere other than work.

The reality is that amidst a malaise of disengagement, with growing disassociation between employer and employee, very few of your people, or even your senior colleagues, will give a moment's thought to this idea of glue.

But what if they did? And you were the reason that they did?

What if you were the one who nurtured that glue?

Think what a difference that could make?

Last words

Glue was written as a kind of paean – sharing my love of executive development and the privilege of being involved amongst those engaged in continuous learning.

I have focused on those organisations, leaders and colleagues whom I know well, and particularly those who exemplified the pursuit of glue. There are numerous others that I don't know, who are busy somewhere trying to provide dynamic leadership and encourage closer collaboration within their firms.

Anyone who has tidied up the messy conference room at the end of a major learning intervention will know that there are few experiences in business life that are more satisfying or memorable. In an age when individualisation is the mode du jour, we should applaud those leaders, educators, facilitators, guest speakers, coaches, contributors and learning practitioners trying to create glue. I have been blessed to have been involved in many learning experiences that have prompted "dongcha" – insights and "aha moments" which have shaped the way leaders think and feel about themselves, their teams, their firms and the future.

Andrew Scott, an economics Professor at LBS and an expert on longevity, recently started one of his classes for a group of senior executives with an enigmatic proposition:

> I do hope at the end of this day that you will feel that you could live your life differently.[6]

For me that sums up the message of this book in one sentence: we need to live our working lives differently. We know deep down that we can only improve our organisations, our workplaces, our colleagues' lives, and our customer's experiences by better harnessing the efforts, ideas and energy of very many other people. Glue is about actively enabling them, through making small but important shifts ourselves, and living our working lives in new ways, so they can experience their working lives differently.

I do not pretend that transforming leadership in this way will be easy. If we try though, the impact will be profound and, perhaps like Jack Ma in his flat Hangzhou, our ambition will be great, the hours will be long, but the reward will be enormous.

Notes and references

1 Quoted by Jeff Bezos, CEO of Amazon (April 2016) from his annual letter to shareholders.

2 Online article: "The Surprising Truth About Amazon and Booking.com's Culture of Experimentation." See: https://www.awa-digital.com/blog/truth-about-amazon-booking-experimentation-culture/

3 Sinek, S. (2011) *Start With Why*. Penguin Books. The quote is from *How Great Leaders Inspire Action* by Simon Sinek, a TED Talk by Sinek from September 2009. Retrieved from: https://www.ted.com/talks/simon_sinek_how_great_leaders_inspire_action

4 Pinker, Susan. (2017) *The Village Effect: How Face-to-Face Contact Can Make us Healthier, Happier, and Smarter*. Atlantic Books.

5 "The secret to living longer may be your social life." Retrieved from a Ted Talk transcript at: https://youtube.com/watch?v=ptIecdCZ3dg&feature=shares. "The research was based on work by Julianne Holt-Lunstad . . . a researcher at Brigham Young University who addressed this very question in a series of studies of tens of thousands of middle-aged people much like this audience here. She looked at every aspect of their lifestyle: their diet, their

exercise, their marital status, how often they went to the doctor, whether they smoked or drank, etc. She recorded all of this and then she and her colleagues sat tight and waited for seven years to see who would still be breathing. And of the people left standing, and what reduced their chances of dying the most? That was her question."

6 The quote is from Professor Andrew, a faculty member at London Business School. He is co-author, with Lynda Gratton. (2016) *The 100-Year Life: Living and Working in an Age of Longevity.* Bloomsbury.

RESOURCES

The following suggests a brief selection of some further reading and online resources. You may enjoy discovering more about the key concepts in this book, including the importance of social capital, organisational culture, authentic leadership, humanocracy, autonomy, experimentation and other key ideas.

A book about glue

You can explore the topic and find more stories about glue at **www. abookaboutglue.com** which includes two online resources: "The Glueometer" is a survey tool to gauge the observed leadership behaviours and other aspects of your firm which gives you a sense of how "tangible" glue is within your organisation. Accompanying this is "The Sniff Test", which is a simple self-diagnostic tool that can help you gauge your own personal approach in creating and nurturing glue.

Social capital

- Robert P. Putnam, *Bowling Alone: The Collapse and Revival of American Community.* (2000) Simon & Schuster.

- Sumantra Ghoshal, and J. Nahapiet, "Social Capital, Intellectual Capital, and the Organizational Advantage", *The Academy of Management Review*, Vol. 23, No. 2 (April 1998), pp. 242–266 (25 pages) Published by: Academy of Management.

Organisations, leadership and culture

- Sumantra Ghoshal and Christopher, *The Individualized Corporation: A Fundamentally New Approach to Management.* (2011) Heinemann.
- Gary Hamel and Michele Zanini, *Humanocracy: Creating Organizations as Amazing as The People Inside Them.* (2020) Harvard Business Review Press. Gary Hamel also shares numerous resources, videos, and articles, at www.garyhamel.com
- Rob Goffee and Gareth Jones, *Why Should Anyone Be Led by You? What It Takes to Be an Authentic Leader.* (2006) Harvard Business Review Press.
- Costantinos C. Markides, *Organizing for New Normal: Prepare Your Company for the journey of Continuous Disruption.* (2021) Kogan Page.
- Peter Hinssen, *The Phoenix and The Unicorn: The Why, What and How of Corporate Innovation.* (2020) nexxworks. For more on the future of work, technology, and organisations, see www.nexxworks.com
- Hugh McLeod, *Ignore Everybody: And 39 Other Keys to Creativity.* (2009) Portfolio.

Galvanising leaders

- Brent Schlender and Rick Tezeli, *Becoming Steve Jobs. The Evolution of a Reckless Upstart into a Visionary Leader.* (2015) Sceptre.
- Duncan Clark, *Alibaba: The House That Jack Ma Built.* (2016) ecco
- Ashlee Vance, *Elon Musk: How the Billionaire CEO of SpaceX and Tesla is Shaping Our Future.* (2015) Virgin.

Customer centricity

- Charlie Dawson, and Seán Meehan, *The Customer Copernicus: How to be Customer-Led.* (2021) Routledge.

Experimentation

- Rob James and Jules Goddard, *Business Experimentation: A Practical Guide for Driving Innovation and Performance in Your Business.* (2021) Kogan Page.
- David J, Bland, Alex Osterwalder, designed by Alan Smith and Trish Papadakos, *Testing Business Ideas.* (2020) Wiley. Colourful and comprehensive guide to dozens of different types of rapid experimentation.

Much of the inspiration for this book came from the leaders I have had the opportunity to work for, but also the hundreds of leaders I have been able to work with while they have attended London Business School. There are numerous LBS resources, ideas, and thought-leadership articles online at www.london.edu/think.

INDEX

Note: Page numbers followed by "n" indicate endnotes.